RENEWING THE COUNTRYSIDE

Minnesota

RENEWING THE COUNTRYSIDE

Minnesota

Editors:
Jan Joannides, Sara Bergan, Mark Ritchie, Beth Waterhouse and Okechukwu Ukaga

Production and Design:
Brett Olson

Senior Writers:
Beth Waterhouse and Tim King

Senior Photographer:
Doug Beasley

Published jointly by the
Institute for Agriculture and Trade Policy
the
Great Plains Institute for Sustainable Development
and the
Northeast Minnesota Sustainable Development Partnership, University of Minnesota

www.mncountryside.org

Renewing the Countryside

Editors

Jan Joannides
Sara Bergan
Mark Ritchie
Beth Waterhouse
Okechukwu Ukaga

Design and Production

Brett Olson, Geografix

Senior Writers

Beth Waterhouse
Tim King

Senior Photographer

Doug Beasley, Beasley Photography

Story Contact Coordinator

Wendi Ward

Printer

A. G. Johnson, Minneapolis, Minnesota, USA

Paper

100 lb. Reincarnation Matte
100% recycled, 50% post consumer waste
New Leaf Paper, San Francisco

Sponsors

The Northwest Area Foundation
Northeast Minnesota Sustainable Development Partnership, University of Minnesota
The McKnight Foundation
The Minnesota Office of Environmental Assistance
The Surdna Foundation
Experiment in Rural Cooperation, University of Minnesota
Minnesota Institute for Sustainable Agriculture, University of Minnesota
Agricultural Utilization Research Institute
North County Co-op

ISBN 0-9713391-0-4 (hardcover); ISBN 0-9713391-1-2 (paperback)

Library of Congress Control Number: 2001095604

First Printing

We dedicate this book
to the individuals and families working each day
to renew Minnesota's countryside.

FOREWORD

Across Minnesota's diverse and beautiful landscape, creative, hard-working people are bringing new energy to the countryside. With perseverance, inventiveness, and occassionally, simple good fortune, they are creating a new definition of what it means to live, work, and learn in rural America. These people are enhancing our state's cultural and natural resources while spurring local economic development in their communities. While their backgrounds and activities differ, each in their own way is renewing the countryside.

In this book, we share the stories of some of these people. We share them to acknowledge and honor their accomplishments. We also share them in hopes that they will inspire others to pursue their dreams of businesses, programs, and partnerships that can enhance both community well-being and the environment.

Furthermore, we hope this book motivates those who want to support rural communities and protect our natural resources to "vote with their dollars." By purchasing goods and services from the enterprises highlighted here, and others like them, readers can do their part to renew the countryside. A map and index at the end of this book make it easy to call, write, or email most of the featured businesses to find out where to obtain their products and services.

Finally, we hope that policymakers and government officials will read this book with care. Although it showcases private initiatives, there are crucial roles that goverment agencies play in helping new ideas and initiatives take root.

The stories selected for this book come from the Renewing the Countryside website (www.mncountryside.org) where information is available on hundreds of initiatives from all over our state. Over the next year, we will add examples from other states and Canada as well. The website is also a place to connect to useful information and resources. Our goal is to support innovative, sustainable development in rural communities in every way possible.

We have produced this book in ways consistent with the values and practices of the people highlighted in these pages. Local writers and photographers provided the content and pictures. A Minnesota, union printer printed this book. The paper used is as environmentally-responsible as is currently available and was purchased from a company committed to environmental stewardship. Even the website software was created here in Minnesota.

The inspiration for this book came from The Netherlands, where the Ministry of Agriculture produced what they called an "atlas" of similar initiatives throughout the Dutch countryside. We graciously acknowledge the gift of this idea from our friends in Europe and hope that our *Renewing the Countryside* book will in turn inspire others to take stock of all the wonderful, creative things being done in their own backyards.

Sincerely,

Mark Ritchie, Sara Bergan, and Jan Joannides

ROOT RIVER MARKET

Witt's Pharmacy

MISSISSIPPI HEADWATERS AYH-HOSTEL

JAVA RIVER

Rural America Arts Center

Angry Trout Cafe

LYNDALE YOUTH FARM MARKET PROJECT

WE WORK TO
GROW HEALTHY FOOD FOR THE COM
BEAUTIFY THE NEIGHBORHOOD
PROVIDE JOBS FOR YOUTH
BRING PEOPLE TOGETHER
Visit Our

PRAIRIE RESTORATION

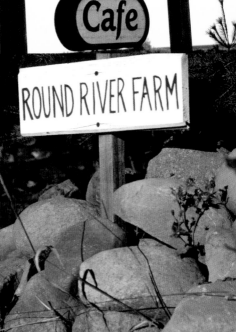

ROUND RIVER FARM

Camphill Bakery

TABLE OF CONTENTS

A special thanks to Olivia

INTRODUCTION

This book is a glimpse into the lives of people creating a resilient, prosperous future for Minnesota. It is a collection of stories about individuals, families and communities protecting the beauty and vitality of our countryside by putting their landscapes to work. With their creativity, determination, and hard work, they are breathing new life and energy into Minnesota's rural communities and protecting the natural and cultural resources that are invaluable to us all.

The great fun of this project was the honor and responsibility of going out into the countryside and asking, "what is working?" The answers to our question come in forms as diverse as the people of our state, as diverse as the ecosystems in which they live.

Hope may be the most important energy needed in the countryside. The editors and writers of this book recognize that as individuals and communities begin to make renewing changes, there is a need for models, ideas, and stories. Details of successful ventures help people believe that what they try will make a difference.

Information has never been more abundant, but real change comes when information joins imagination on the particular piece of land that we may inhabit. Locally, farm by farm or community by community, we must look at what we are given and take it from there. We can only create from the here and now.

These stories are written to save people energy and time. They are written to entertain and to lend hope. You will read about soil and tree, vegetables and prairie flowers, as well as human ingenuity, hospitality and generosity. If you need ideas, or if you love to read of the innovation and creativity of the human mind and spirit, then you have picked up the right book. Read on.

CHAPTER ONE
Farming

Motivations vary in these creative farming stories. Observing exactly where the water flows, watching soil blow off the landscape, or knowing the dangers of chemicals and large equipment — all are motivating factors as farmers renew their practices and their land. After decades of cheap food policies, which have put many farms out of business, the words farming and ingenuity now often fall in the same sentence. Creativity helps keep people on the land.

Here — describing native grass seed and Swedish hog houses, or sweet corn stands everywhere — are stories of successful farming at this, the turn of our century. Farmers re-establish prairie for wildlife, use reindeer droppings to grow tomatoes, or nurture anxious hogs by giving them space. Each piece of land calls for its own solutions, and ingenuity is the common thread running through these five stories. Farmers see what they gain and lose with choices on each farmstead, and demonstrate the best of human adaptability as a factor within the ecology of place.

WILLOW LAKE FARM
Farming with New Eyes

Tony Thompson likes to take pictures of his corn and soybean fields during rainstorms. He does it so he can learn how the water moves across the fields. "Nothing substitutes for actually being there during a storm," he says.

Tony has lived on his family's Willow Lake Farm, near Windom, Minnesota, all of his life. Although he holds a bachelor's degree in Agronomy and has continued post-graduate studies in Plant Community Ecology from Montana State University at Bozeman, he really never left home for school. "I went to school winter quarter for sixteen years," Tony explains, "but when they adopted the semester system, it created a conflict with my farming." For Tony, farming took precedence.

"The voyage lies not in seeking new lands, but in seeing with new eyes," noted philosopher Marcel Proust. For Tony, school was a place for learning to see Willow Lake Farm, and the southwestern Minnesota countryside, through more informed eyes. Tony explains, "I remember taking a botany class when I was twenty-one and the only wildflowers I knew then in southwestern Minnesota were the pasque flower, the blue flag iris, and maybe the violet." Today, Tony can identify over 200 species of plants that live on or near his farm. College allowed his eyes to see the farm in the way his heart always did; now he can take a camera into his corn and soybean fields during a rainstorm and understand what he is seeing.

Thanks to those soggy photo sessions, Tony has placed grass waterways and filter strips in the best locations to prevent erosion on his 1600 acres of corn and soybean fields. In 1991, he adapted his

fields to a ridge tillage system, a reduced tillage system where crops are planted on permanent ridges. This system enables the soil to absorb water, rather than letting it run off into nearby streams, ditches, and wetlands. "We've learned that there's less than one quarter of the runoff water coming from the ridge till fields compared to those tilled conventionally. When that water finally does come, it's much cleaner — there's much less soil and attached herbicides and fertilizers in the runoff water," Tony explains.

Recently, with help from the Minnesota Department of Agriculture's Energy and Sustainable Agriculture Grant Program, Tony has been trying to increase the diversity of plants in his corn and soybean fields, so he can even better protect the soil. Using a specially designed seeder he has been able to experiment with planting red clover, annual alfalfa, annual rye grass, hairy vetch, and buckwheat right amidst the living corn and soybeans. His idea is to have something growing in the soil as close to year-round as possible. "As

farmers, we've skewed our whole soil ecology," Tony says. "If we want to do something to make the soil ecology more diverse, so that a disease like soybean cyst nematode will have a tougher time, we should add elements to the crop rotation that won't hurt corn and soybean yields."

Tony is interested in diversity for reasons beyond good crop yields. "I've been seeing a lot of upland sandpipers in the soybeans," Tony notes, "and not just individuals, but broods." These successful sandpiper broods in his soybean fields please Tony. They would have pleased his father too. "My dad went to a lot of Audubon and other conservation meetings and, as a kid, I'd tag along," Tony remembers. "My interest just grew. I wasn't so much interested in hunting, like my dad and the other older farmers; I was more interested in agronomy and plant ecology."

Tagging along with his father, reading his great aunt's copy of Aldo Leopold's *Sand County Almanac*, or associating with older farmers from the neighborhood have influenced how Tony Thompson sees the land and his place on it. It was, in many ways, his love for these people and their connection to the land that kept him from leaving the farm.

"When I was in college, a neighboring farmer wanted me to work with him. He was just a wonderful guy — an unusual sort of farmer that we don't have many of now," Tony says. "He was a good corn and soybean farmer, but he also had this huge interest in birds and hunting and trapping. When we were kids," Tony remembers, "he'd come in the early morning and he'd drop some animal in our bed to get us up! He always had some squirming creature in a gunnysack in the back of his pick-up truck." These associations and connections, along with Tony's sixteen winters at school in Bozeman, fostered his interest and love of the prairie and the wild animals that inhabit it.

Over a period of many years, Tony has been able to turn this interest in preserving remnants of southwestern Minnesota's tall grass prairie into a

profitable part of his enterprise. "After I took my first field botany class, I realized the tall grass prairie is a tremendously diverse plant community," Tony says. "I started renting land from a great aunt, my dad, and some cousins who had remnant prairies on their land. These were mostly old native hayfields or pastures."

Some of the pastures, although never plowed, were overcome with invasive thistles. Native prairie plants were scarce. In an effort to control the rampant thistles and restore the prairie, Tony started to experiment with fire and biological controls. He also tried to graze the pastures rotationally with cattle. The grazing failed, and he never made money on the cattle, but the fire and biological controls worked. The thistles largely disappeared and the native plant diversity skyrocketed.

Over fifteen years ago, Tony started experimenting with harvesting the seeds from his prairie. "Now I've got a huge seed crop," he says. "This last year, we collected thousands of pounds of seeds." Tony uses an old John Deere combine to harvest from August through October — he gets different species for each season — and sells the crop to the Minnesota and Iowa Departments of Natural Resources and to fellow farmers who plant the seed on land they have in the Conservation Reserve Program.

Tony is glad to have an economic reason to protect the prairie. He is even more delighted to have provided a haven for a multitude of prairie plants, birds, and furry, squirming creatures on his land. Whether it is in his fields of corn and soybeans or his tall grass prairie, Tony is caring for his land and making a living in a way that would make his dad, and all his old farmer friends, proud.

PASTURES A PLENTY
Taking the Anxiety out of Farming

In 1988, as wind swept soil away from the VanDerPols' dry fields near Kerkhoven, Minnesota, LeeAnn VanDerPol sadly watched from a window and then stepped outside to take photographs. "When we were looking at the pictures later, we decided we didn't want to continue to farm the way we were farming — that there had to be a better way," recalls LeeAnn.

That was a turning point for LeeAnn and her husband Jim. They began to make a transition to more sustainable farming methods. "It wasn't an easy decision to make," LeeAnn remarks. "It's scary. You're afraid you'll lose everything." "Faster than you might, anyway," adds Jim. "But if we hadn't changed our way of farming, we likely would not be here now."

The VanDerPols raise 320 acres of diversified crops and pasture, in support of several livestock operations, with their son and daughter-in-law, Josh and Cindy. Their farm, Pastures A Plenty, is home to a hog-farrowing operation, a replacement dairy heifer business, and pastured chickens.

After twenty years of raising hogs in confinement, a practice where animals are restricted to small spaces within a larger building, the VanDerPols switched to outdoor pork production. They now raise about 1500 hogs a year using the alternative system. They have since taken what many consider old-style hog raising practices and given them a modern technological twist. They use a combination of portable structures for outdoor farrowing (birthing of pigs) in summer pastures. The pasture is divided into four sections, and pigs are periodically rotated to new pasture.

After weaning, young pigs move to hoop houses — large metal-framed, vinyl-covered, semi-circular structures — to continue their growth while the sows stay in the pasture for breeding. "Pasturing and grazing is really environmentally and farmer friendly," comments Jim. "The work is much more pleasant, especially when it comes to the hogs. They're a completely different animal when they're on the grass. You take a lot of anxiety out of pigs by giving them space."

In the winter, all the pigs live in the hoop housing. The VanDerPols rediscovered this hoop house system of raising hogs through research and visits with swine producers from Sweden. Originally developed in Canada, these structures are durable in the winter and allow a great deal of air movement in the summer. The plastic covering holds up well in the winter, shedding snow as the plastic moves in the wind. According to the VanDerPols, the hoop housing is inexpensive and versatile. The building measures 30-feet by 72-feet and can house 200 adult pigs. The building has a dirt floor with deep straw bedding, except for the feeding area that has a concrete floor.

The VanDerPols have a renewed enthusiasm for farming. A demonstration grant from the Minnesota Department of Agriculture's Energy and Sustainable Agriculture Grant Program to graze gilts (young female pigs) and pasture farrows gave the VanDerPols a new start. The hoop building, self-feeder, and concrete feeding area cost a total of $13,000.

Jim, who was thinking about phasing out livestock because his farrowing house needed extensive upgrading, has found many benefits to the hoop housing. Less physical labor is required, and there is less dust and noise than in confinement situations. Combining pasture with these houses is a good way to raise pigs with little expense. "We figure we can produce these pigs for about thirty cents a pound, including labor," Jim contends. "That is less than what it would cost us to raise them in a confinement system."

As for the end product, the VanDerPols are offering an alternative to the standardized, antibiotic-laden products found in grocery stores. As LeeAnn explains, "The animal's diet really makes a difference. Growth hormones make the meat taste different. Many of our customers swear they can taste the confinement in the pork that they buy from the supermarket. Our meat is better tasting because the animals have more freedom."

Instead of letting the market dictate their prices, LeeAnn, Jim, Josh, and Cindy are finding their own specialty markets. Jim explains, "For us, there is no future in the commodity market." The VanDerPols direct-market to customers in neighboring towns, sell their meat at Holy Trinity Lutheran Church in Minneapolis, and make home deliveries by prearrangement. Pastures A Plenty also sells to Niman's Ranch, a company that will only buy hogs that were not fed antibiotics, hormones, or animal by-products, and were raised in an environmentally sound manner. Then there are sales to the local café, on the Internet through www.prairiefare.com, and most recently through a premium export program.

For the VanDerPols, changing their method of farming has had many benefits. They enjoy farming more. The animals are happier. And their operation is financially more stable because they are not as vulnerable to the swings in the commodity markets. The VanDerPols can visibly see the improvements in the ecosystem on their farm, too. They have more birds, more wildlife, and the grasses in the pastures hold the soil in place. They no longer worry about the wind sweeping their soil away.

ROUND RIVER FARM

Living Sustainably in the North Woods

Round River Farm and Shalom Seed Sanctuary are nestled in the lap of the Sawtooth Mountains a mile and a half from the North Shore of Lake Superior. Half of the year, you cannot drive up the steep driveway, so you have to walk.

But when you climb the hill, round the bend, and see the stone and timber-framed barn, the windmills, the cliff rising to the east, and the sunny fields spreading southward from the home, you understand. Peace settles over you.

Round River Farm is the home of David and Lise Abazs, and their sons, Colby and Tremayne. Both David and Lise grew up wanting to farm. They met in college, and during their last year of school traveled to many parts of the world learning about farming through an independent study program. After they were married, Lise and David spent six months in New Mexico at the High Desert Research Farm. It was there that they learned about seed saving, an interest that grew into the Shalom Seed Sanctuary — a non-profit organization they have formed to provide education and preserve heirloom varieties of seeds.

Virtually every step they take in their life, every product they buy, every improvement they make on their house and land, is based on their decision to live by the cycles of nature and to "tread lightly on the earth." Lise and David incorporate the lessons of the surrounding wilderness into their lives to create a sustainably balanced existence with their environment. "On our forty acres, we strive to maintain a maximum diversity of domestic animals and crops, as well as wildlife," says David. "Our needs are met by harnessing animal, solar, wind, and people power, and by harvesting the cultivated and natural bounties of the earth."

One of the Abazs' goals is to be self-sufficient in supplying all of their energy needs. They use solar and wind power to generate electricity. Eight 90- to 100-watt solar panels capture the sun's energy and generate electricity, which is stored in sixteen six-volt deep cycle batteries. The capacity of the system is 2000 watts per day in the summer and half of that during the winter. To meet their projected future needs of 3000 watts per day, they installed a wind generator.

The Abazs family started their farm with an emphasis on animal production, but soon realized that distance from markets, processing, feedstock, and other resources made it difficult to run a successful livestock business. They noticed the scarce supply of fresh, locally-grown vegetables and fruits in their part of the state and decided to concentrate on these products. They now have fruit trees, an acre of vegetable gardens, an 840 square-foot hoop greenhouse, a 10,000 square foot strawberry patch, and 300 blueberry bushes. These plants are watered by an irrigation system that uses rainwater collected from the barn, home, and cabin roofs and well water pumped by a water windmill.

David and Lise learned early about the challenges of growing vegetables in northern Minnesota on marginal soils. Their garden did not produce at all their first year. David comments, "It was discouraging, but after adding tons of manure, ash, and limestone, we now have peas that grow taller than our heads." To build up their thin soils, they use ample additions of reindeer droppings that they get from a farm down the road.

The vegetable garden follows a planned five-year crop rotation and uses raised beds (mounds of soil). Raised beds allow the soil to warm up faster, stay drier during wet years, and enable the plants to send their roots deeper. The crop rotation is based on plant families and soil pH. The rotation includes a cover crop (grains), legumes (peas and beans), brassicas (broccoli, cabbage and kohlrabi), miscellaneous (carrots and onions), and solanaceae (potatoes). The rotation cycle avoids disease build-up in the soil and makes efficient use of nutrients.

Three varieties of blueberries are grown in extensive patches — North Blue, North Country and North Sky. All were developed by the University of Minnesota to combine cold-hardiness traits with heavy yields. The quarter-acre strawberry patch includes both Glooscap and Cavendish varieties, which bear their fruit in early July. The Abazs family also keeps bees and raises goats, sheep, and ducks.

It took ten years for the gardens to turn a profit, but today the operation makes money. The Abazs farm supplies thirty families with healthy, fresh food each week through their Community Supported Agriculture program. By minimizing inputs and getting full value for their products through direct marketing, they are able to maximize their profits. Other on-farm income comes from selling Christmas trees and marketing and selling alternative energy systems and gray water treatment system kits. Lise also has a part-time, off-farm job which provides a form of "crop insurance" and extra income for trips, savings, and retirement.

David explains, "Instead of holding high-income jobs, we put sweat equity into our buildings, farm, and home. Now we have a variety of ways to generate income. The big motivating factor for us is getting good quality food we can trust."

NEW IMMIGRANT FARM PROGRAM
The Changing Face of Agriculture

In the Nineteenth and early Twentieth centuries, the Johnsons and Nelsons and Olsons were immigrants to Minnesota, typically farmers from Scandinavia who displaced the Dakota and Ojibwe who were here before them. The new immigrants to Minnesota are named Hernández and Nguyen and Faduma and Vang. They are from Mexico, Somalia, Ethiopia, and Laos, to name a few countries. U.S. Census figures for 2000 have borne out what by now is obvious to most Minnesotans: the face of the state is changing, not to mention the names.

The Minnesota Department of Planning estimates that upwards of 224,000 new immigrants live in the state. Many are refugees. They seek not to displace anyone but to fit peacefully into a geographical and social landscape that is foreign in many ways. A large number of new immigrants have agrarian backgrounds but are constrained to living in the Twin Cities. For some who seek a familiar relationship with the land, the University of Minnesota Extension Service's New Immigrant Farm Program offers an opportunity.

Partners from the various immigrant communities help the University find the farmers, and extension staff help them increase their vegetable production efficiency. "Even though they have agrarian backgrounds, they're not familiar with farming in this country," says Nigatu Tadesse, extension educator and coordinator of the program. "We're trying to improve their marketing techniques and production so they will be profitable in their businesses."

Most of the 140 or so participant farmers are Hmong or Hispanic. Almost all sell their harvest at area farmers' markets, and the effort is a family affair from field to market. Khue Vang is a Hmong farmer in the program. Khue, along with three brothers, used to farm pickles for Gedney. He now owns a thirteen-acre farm in Stacy and rents an additional ten acres in Hugo. "We do small-scale farming with a variety of Oriental vegetables," says Khue, who came to the United States in 1976, "plus we have

The New Immigrant Farm Program works with immigrants in the seven-county metropolitan area who have chosen farming as their occupation and who already own or lease land, usually between one and twenty acres.

greenhouses to take care of community needs for special vegetable plants and herbs that the nurseries around here can't grow." One corner of a greenhouse is reserved for Khue's mother, who grows about fifteen herbs "in the traditional way," including an herb Khue dubs "manplant." "It's just like — what do they call it — Viagra™?" he quips.

Khue appreciates the advice extension educators provide for rotating crops and post-harvest handling, but points out that Hmong farmers have difficulties acquiring adequate machinery, let alone good land. "We want to rent land, but the problem is that the good land is already taken, and the available land isn't good enough for vegetables."

Extension educators also face challenges in their work with new immigrants. "It's delicate when you're working with people from different cultural backgrounds to know how to talk to the female and how to talk to the male," says Nigatu. "It's not proper to shake ladies' hands. We have to know not only the science, but also the culture…. And they have to know who you are and build trust."

The University of Minnesota's Extension Service, which partners in these new immigrant programs with groups like the Minnesota Food Association, the Minnesota Department of Agriculture, and the United States Department of Agriculture Farm Services Agency, is committed to its outreach mission, especially for new immigrants and communities of color. "From our inception, we've been doing that — empowering those at the margins," says Juan Moreno, diversity and inclusion specialist for the Extension Service. In the latter part of the Nineteenth century, the needs of peasant immigrant farmers coming mainly from Europe were "primarily in literacy and leadership," Juan says. "The Extension Service has always been about generating capacity in all kinds of literacies including civic literacy and leadership — that's what allows you to access the corridors of power, ultimately."

In addition to the New Immigrant Program, the Extension Service also runs a Farming Incubator Program. This program, targeted to new immigrants who do not have land, helps individuals and families make the transition into sustainable, small-scale farming operations by leasing them parcels of land for up to four years at the University's Rosemount Research and Outreach Center. The program also provides classroom and field-based educational activities. "We have some crops that there's no English name for," notes David Walgenbach, director of operations at the Rosemount Research and Outreach Center. "A different form of agriculture will surround the metro area in the future because of growing diversity."

The new immigrants are likely to offer their Scandinavian predecessors a new way of looking at things, as well as a few new items for the grocery cart. Immigrants are now growing teff, a staple grain in East Africa used for making bread, as well as different varieties of sorghum and eggplant. One plant, which is considered a weed by most farmers, is used by the Hmong people as an ingredient in soup. Through programs like these, new immigrants have an opportunity to connect with their traditions and generate wealth for their families. "These people — they have so much attachment to the soil that it's therapeutic," Nigatu says. "People who are 80, they come to the field and it gives them relief — both physically and psychologically. It is a way of life for these people to work in the field. And it brings the family together."

PETERSON FAMILY FARM
Farming with Family and Imagination

Sever Peterson is among the third generation to farm his family's land in the Minnesota River Valley in Eden Prairie. An extended Peterson family has always been involved in the farm since Sever's grandfather acquired it in the 1880s. In the 1930s, when highways 212 and 169 were being built, the Peterson Brothers' Produce built their first retail stand at a location now called Lion's Tap, on the highway at the bottom of Flying Cloud Hill.

"Since the turn of the century, our family has been very involved at the Minneapolis Farmers' Market," Sever says. They grow sweet corn, melons, tomatoes, cucumbers, and pumpkins. In Sever's mind, the Peterson Farm remains a vegetable farm after all of these years, although more than half of its 1000 acres is dedicated to corn and soybeans.

The entire family is still involved in the operation. "I have five siblings," Sever says, "and all of my nieces and nephews, and their spouses, either work or have worked on our farm. They've worked in the field, at the retail stands, and some at the computer." That has been very gratifying to Sever, his wife, Sharon, his siblings, and their spouses. But the next generation is growing past the farm. "That's a lament," says Sever. "They've gotten their education, are qualified to do other work, and they've gone on to do that."

Other changes have transpired. Up until the 1960s, Sever's father and uncle had excellent relationships with the produce buyers of the small groceries they served. Then the "Mom and Pop" groceries began to disappear, and the food business began a pattern of consolidation that has continued to this day. The produce buyers at the little stores, the ones that knew the Peterson kids by name, began to be replaced by buyers whose only goal was to buy the cheapest product they could. "I recall conversations at our supper table that some of these buyers were only concerned with rock bottom prices, no matter what," explains Sever. "And in that classical economic relationship, other elements — like respect, honesty, and appreciation — were lost."

At that time, the Petersons made the decision to stop selling to grocers and to market directly to retail customers. These days, customers looking for fresh

products can find the Petersons' produce at stands throughout the southern and western suburbs of the Twin Cities and at the Minneapolis Farmers' Market.

And while Sever says simply, "I'm a vegetable farmer," he grows hundreds of acres of corn and soybeans. "The main reason I keep growing field corn and soybeans is because it allows me to keep in touch with the harsh realities of commodity agriculture," explains Sever. Firsthand knowledge gives him

credibility when he discusses agricultural policy with other farmers. "It is economic folly and a social tragedy what is happening in the commodity side of agriculture," he says. "And these issues go back 40 to 50 years."

There is another reason the Petersons remain among the few cash-grain farmers left in principally urban Hennepin County. Sever's sense of himself and his family is tied to the land and his family's history on it. "I grew up as a farmer, and growing grain is a part of farming that I love. It's a time when my family and I can be involved in the operation by ourselves," says Sever. "When we do the planting, we do it as a family. When it comes time to harvest, we do that as a family too. When we work together, we play off the same sheet of music — it's a beautiful sound."

The Peterson farm has been able to hang onto its grain operation against the odds, but the livestock went a long time ago. "We sold the last cattle two days before I left for Vietnam," Sever remembers. "We had a cow-calf operation, and I miss those animals to this day."

One of the family's recent projects is a corn maze. The idea originated when an English foreign exchange student stayed with the Peterson family in the early 1970s. The student explained that mazes were common in the ancient gardens of English castles, and they went as far back as Greek mythology when the hero Theseus slew the Minotaur and escaped the darkness of the Cretan maze by rewinding a magical ball of golden yarn.

The Petersons were intrigued, but did not do anything about it until 1997. That year, they designed a Tyrannosaurus Rex maze. Since then the family has created the *Titanic*, an enchanted castle, and, in the spring of 2000, The Nation's Capitol maze. President Bill Clinton even came out to visit that one in May of 2000.

The maze is a well-organized family event. Maze travelers are given an orientation and a map before they enter the maze, and security people tirelessly monitor the maze's seven footpaths so that no one becomes lost. When travelers exit the maze, they can feast on roasted sweet corn and be serenaded by live music.

Overseeing a crew to run the busy maze, and sometimes their 15-acre pumpkin patch, is a lot of work for Sever, Sharon, and their family.

But they enjoy these times. They enjoy seeing grandparents, parents, and children coming together to take pleasure in the fruits of their family's labor. In many ways, that is what farming is about.

While the family continues to respond creatively to increasing challenges in the marketplace, Sever remains concerned that the suburbs may eventually engulf the family farm. Although much of the farm is in the Minnesota River Valley and beyond the direct reach of sprawl, he is haunted by visions of creeping subdivisions. "That's one of the most difficult questions in my mind," he says. "For me, home has never been anywhere else."

SCHERPING FAMILY FARM

The Difference Grazing Makes

Rick and June Scherping, two Stearns County farmers, have made seeking quality of life for their family, the profitability of their farm, and stewardship of the land a complete whole. They do not separate the parts. "We farm this way because of the quality of life it gives our family," Rick and June explain.

The Scherpings, in using intensive rotational grazing on their 200-acre dairy farm, are in the midst of a revolution that has spread across livestock-producing areas of the United States in the last decade. In addition to being part of what many people are calling "grass-based farming," the Scherpings are also part of the booming market for organic dairy products. In 1999, their farm became certified organic. "Our milk prices held steady during the end of 2000 and the beginning of 2001, while non-organic prices were often below the cost it took to produce the milk," Rick reports. Now the Scherpings' way of life has created a nicely profitable enterprise and they have the solid financial numbers that prove it.

For the Scherpings, like so many other experienced farmers, the shift toward rotational grazing and organic farming started when they began to notice something was wrong on their farm. Fifteen years ago, Rick and his family farmed in a conventional manner. Rick plowed the black soil on his farm each season and purchased big bags of chemically-treated corn from the seed companies. He grew the corn, and harvested it with expensive, dangerous equipment. Then he hauled it to his silo and barn to feed his cows. The corn required chemical fertilizers and costly herbicides, and Rick saw increasing numbers of warnings printed on the labels of products he had originally been told were perfectly safe.

As a result, Rick and his family began to question their farming techniques. Should they continue to buy these expensive and potentially dangerous chemicals? Did it make sense to use heavy machinery around the children, or even adults? Was plowing the soil each season, and watching some of it wash away each time you plowed, the right way to be stewards of the land?

After careful thought, the Scherpings' answers were no, no, and NO! And so they began the adventure toward grass and organic farming. Since they made the decision to switch to a grass-based system, they have planted a little more acreage into permanent pasture and hayfields each year, and a little less into cornfields. "A couple of years ago, the farm reached a point where there was no longer a bare field on the land," says Rick. "During the growing season, everywhere you look there is a thick, lush mat of green." That means, for much of the year, Rick lets the cows do the harvesting instead of driving around in expensive equipment planting and then gathering up crops to haul to the cows.

Now Rick, June, or even the older children rotate the farm's 62 milking cows from one small pasture or paddock to another, once or twice a day. Rick enjoys taking one of the three young Guatemalan children he and June adopted along on these trips. "When you walk out to move the cows, you can study the animals' behavior and the quality of the grass," he says. "You can

listen to and understand your farm better than when you are in an air-conditioned tractor cab. And you can get to know your children better!"

By moving the cows quickly over the grass they only graze the most nutritious part, and the grass does not become over-grazed like it would if the cows were left in the same pasture for weeks on end. Grass allowed to rest like this develops healthy root systems and can more readily survive central Minnesota's dry summers. When it does rain, farmers have discovered that well-managed pastures absorb more water than cornfields or continuously-grazed pastures. This means less muddy run-off water flows into nearby creeks and lakes. Rotationally grazed pastures also provide more wildlife habitat than cornfields.

Rotational grazing is largely a system of agriculture developed by farmers. That it works at all has surprised most of the experts. The financial results of the system particularly dumbfounded economists and livestock experts who had been telling farmers that the only way to make a living on a dairy farm was to do whatever it took to get higher yields. This often meant keeping the cows inside and taking out enormous loans to invest in the necessary equipment. Farmers using a grass-based system know better. Even before the Scherping farm went organic, the dairy was showing net results equal to or better than the confinement dairies being promoted by universities and state departments of agriculture.

On a grass-fed livestock farm, cows are healthier, so there are fewer veterinary expenses. Since large machinery is not required, fuels costs are lower. Interest payments to bankers and machinery costs are reduced. Seed and herbicide costs are reduced or eliminated. And, although grass-fed cows produce less milk than confined corn-fed cows, the net profits on farms like the Scherpings' are as good as or better than on confinement farms.

When the Scherpings did the numbers in 2000, their first full year of organic production, results were even better than they expected. Rick compared the

Scherpings' farm results with the 1999 averages of 564 dairy farms in the 1999 Minnesota Farm Business Management Programs Annual Report. The Scherpings had a gross income of $125,000 compared to the average farm in the Report, which had $180,000. Their farm, however, had less than half the direct expenses — $54,000 compared to $107,000, and overhead costs of $8000 compared to the average overhead of $19,000.

"We did these numbers in December," Rick admits, "so we had to estimate the last month." His last month's estimates were pretty accurate. Although the Scherping's farm produced less milk, their expenses, which were fifty percent of their gross income, left them with $63,000. The average confinement dairy, with its exclusive emphasis on high production, spent seventy-five percent of their gross income on direct and overhead costs, thus leaving those operations with $53,000.

For Rick and June, farming is more than just being profitable. The rotational grazing system, with its absence of farm chemicals and heavy equipment, is a safe place to raise a family. It has created more family time, too. "The reason we so enjoy our way of farming is that we are able to understand God's creation in a better way and enjoy His gift of children to the fullest," says Rick. This was important to Rick and June in raising their first four children, Jenny, Rachel, Travis, and Jeremy, who are now nearly all adults, and continues to be important in raising the new additions to their family, Mishel, Victor, and Rodolfo.

CHAPTER TWO
Marketing

If there is a market, there can be creativity in a business or farming operation, and sustainable practices as well. This is not just to sustain the water that runs through the creeks and through our veins, nor is it just to sustain the black soil under our feet — the base of all life. This is to keep people on the land, tilling the soil and raising the livestock. This is to bring new people to the land and into small communities.

Whether this means delivering farm fresh eggs to church refrigerators, driving homemade goat chevre to the Farmers' Market on Saturdays, or gathering around gourmet coffee on the prairie, these stories will open minds and creative hearts to new ways of thinking about the farmer/consumer connection. Sure, direct marketing reinvents the wheel of food distribution. It also brings the consumer sharply into focus in the farmer/producer's mind while it reminds the consumer of the critical place of the farm in human and community health. A circle completes itself.

WHOLE FARM COOPERATIVE
Eating — A Sacred Exercise

Whole Farm Cooperative sells vegetables, grains, meat, eggs, cheese, maple syrup, and a myriad of other products produced by about fifty family farms in Central Minnesota.

Rural Minnesota has a deep tradition of farmers marketing cooperatively. The democratic impulse of farmers controlling their own destiny by owning businesses jointly, however, was increasingly becoming a sham by the time most Whole Farm Co-op members reached early adulthood; multinational conglomerates had absorbed the small, locally-controlled cooperatives. Management decisions were made far away by strangers in suits, and those decisions were adversely affecting the viability of small farm agriculture.

In an attempt to recapture the spirit of cooperatives, the livestock, dairy, and vegetable farmers wanting a better price for their products formed their own cooperative with a commitment to staying closely involved in its management. Whole Farm Cooperative started in a basement in 1997. In its first year, the co-op sold $30,000 worth of products. In its third year, sales rose to $250,000 — and it moved to a bigger basement. Co-op members get between seventy and eighty-five percent of the retail value of the food they sell. For livestock producers, that is a sixty percent improvement over regular commodity marketing channels.

"We sell our food based on the principle that our customer should know as much as possible about the food — whether it's an onion, T-bone steak, or jug of maple syrup," says Herman Hendrickson, co-op board member. To accomplish this, the co-op has a newsletter, a web page (www.wholefarmcoop.com) with profiles of their farmers, and

they regularly invite customers to field days and celebrations. "Being actively transparent in our farming practices and processing activities has been both time consuming and expensive," says Herman. "Since we've had significant financial assistance from the U.S. and Minnesota Departments of Agriculture, as well as the Agricultural Utilization Research Institute, it is not entirely clear yet whether we can afford to have the close relationships with our customers that we do."

Whole Farm Cooperative has a number of marketing initiatives — they sell to restaurants, neighborhood grocers, neighborhood groups, and the staffs of nonprofit organizations. Their most successful effort has been their "CSA" effort — that's Congregationally Supported Agriculture, not Community Supported Agriculture. As of 2001, the Co-op had established relationships with twelve congregations in the Twin Cities area.

Here is how it works. Someone from a congregation contacts Whole Farm Cooperative because they've heard of them through word-of-mouth referrals, media coverage or advocates of the program. Relationships with congregations take different forms, but no congregation has ever started ordering food from Whole Farm Co-op without a personal visit or two to the church. Co-op members have spoken from the pulpit about their cooperative and made presentations to Peace and Justice Committees. Potlucks,

bazaars, Bible study groups, and church festivals have all been venues for explaining the values and processes of the Whole Farm Cooperative.

The message, in different words, is always the same: customers and farmers are equal partners in agriculture. Eating is inseparable from agriculture, and it

is a sacred exercise. Co-op members tell the congregation about how they protect the land and care for the animals. They talk about having diverse farms in an attempt to mirror natural systems. "And always, these urban people respond with warmth and communicate their own needs," says Herman. "They need to know that what they are eating is good for the earth and that what comes from the earth is good for them." This is the basis for the farm-to-church partnership.

Once a congregation signs on, the logistics are straightforward. Whole Farm Cooperative delivers to the church once a month on a predetermined day. Two weeks before delivery, customers receive, usually by email, an updated price and product list. Customers send their orders to the co-op by an agreed upon deadline. The food (and invoices) are delivered to freezers and refrigerators

in the church in bags with customers' names on them. Customers and volunteers or staff at each church agree on a time when people can pick up their orders. Finally, customers send the co-op a check.

"The rest is just details, two of which are critical to making the system work," explains Herman. Big detail number one — a dedicated volunteer or staff person at the church is essential. That person serves as an organizer and a cheerleader. They distribute price lists to parishioners without email and help track down lost orders. "These 'site coordinators' are saints, and the co-op couldn't do this without them," remarks Herman.

Big detail number two — on the co-op's end, somebody has to receive, organize, and fill all the orders. Whole Farm Co-op has a paid sales represen-

tative who answers the myriad of email questions promptly, signs up new customers, and tracks down the lost carton of eggs. Friendly and timely customer relations are essential. "It is much less expensive to keep a customer than to find a new one," explains Herman.

The co-op cannot yet afford to hire a full-time manager, so they have a management team. They pay three board of director members eight dollars an hour to meet weekly to solve problems and address issues. This team takes care of everything, including inventory issues, new product introductions, and delivery problems. They have hired an operations manager and sales represen-tative that also attend the meetings.

Management, however, requires hours and hours of volunteer time. Herman says, "Running a cooperative business requires passionate commitment, good friends, luck, creativity, business sense, and some unnameable elements that border on craziness." Despite the craziness, the members, customers and staff at Whole Farm Cooperative are determined to have a close connection between those who grow the food and those who eat it.

It is true that Minnesota has a strong cooperative history. It is also true that many Minnesota citizens recognize the sacredness of food. Whole Farm Cooperative's CSA work is based on the concept that food — eating it, and growing it — is an exercise in spirituality. They don't know altogether what that means, but they approach their customers and themselves believing that food is spiritual stuff.

DANCING WINDS FARM
Quality Begets Quality

Mary Doerr did not intend to be a goat farmer. When she purchased her twenty-acre farm in Kenyon, Minnesota, in 1985, her plan was to grow organic produce. She did this, but only for a short while — then along came Ida and Yogurt.

Ida and Yogurt were the first of what was to become a thriving herd of goats at Dancing Winds Farm. These two goats arrived pregnant from a neighbor who no longer wanted them. Soon, Mary had more than she had bargained for. Within a year of buying the farm, she had nine goats and plenty of milk at her disposal. "I was using the milk in all my cooking, making yogurt and ice cream, and I still had more milk than I could use," Mary remembers.

It was time for something new. Time for an enterprise that made use of all of the excess milk her goats produced. "I bought a book about 'cheese-making made easy' and started making cheese in my kitchen," Mary recalls. Everything was experimental at first, and there were bad batches to accompany the batches that turned out really well.

It did not take long for Mary to begin marketing her cheese. After sampling her product, the organic distributor that bought her vegetables offered to buy all of the cheese she could make. Finally, in 1987, after juggling the organic produce and the herd, she switched her attention to the goats. "I like everything about the goats," she says, "their intelligence, their mischief. They are social creatures, and they don't do what you want them to do. They don't just follow like sheep." For some, this would be a recipe for disaster, but Mary has found a perfect fit. Her customers are glad she chose the trade!

"I am keeping a lost art alive," explains Mary. "The people who are willing to make cheese in small batches, who work with milk and willingly hang onto that art form, are few." Integral to the quality of her cheese, which comes in many different styles and flavors, is the lifestyle of the goats. "The key to successful cheese-making," says Mary, "is healthy and happy goats. Your cheese is only as good as your milk, and your milk is only as good as your goats."

At Dancing Winds Farm, Mary produces artisan cheeses such as feta, chevre, Gouda, Camembert, and other French-style cheeses. Blocks of feta are available in plain, sun-dried tomato and basil, and other creative flavors. Her signature cheese is a fresh chevre called Bombay Button, after the unofficial name of the community, Bombay, in which she lives. Mary also sells logs of fresh chevre plain, rolled in Herbs de Provence, garlic and dill, Oriental seasoning with ginger, and Thai seasoning with pineapple. Customers rave about her cheeses, and she regularly sells out at the St. Paul Farmers' Market. Mary also sells her cheese directly from Dancing Winds Farm.

Currently, Mary milks twelve goats twice daily, producing around 100 pounds of cheese weekly. To make chevre, she pasteurizes the milk, and when it is cool, adds bacterial culture and enzymes to promote the formation of curds. After the milk mixture incubates, the curds (the solid part) are separated from the whey (the liquid). The curds are shaped and drained in cheesecloth. Fresh chevre is ready after five to seven days. Aged chevre is cured for two to eight weeks.

The goat breeds in Mary's herd produce milk with between two and four percent fat, resulting in a naturally low-fat cheese. Mary uses a vegetable-derived enzyme instead of animal-derived enzymes (rennet) in the cheesemaking. This makes the final product edible to vegetarians and non-vegetarians alike. Some people also find they can eat goat cheese even if they cannot eat cow's milk cheese because it is more easily digested. Mary has also opted to make her cheese lower in sodium. While most feta is cured in brine that is twenty percent salt, Mary cures hers in brine that is only four percent salt. Her fresh chevre is "no salt added" and only a little salt is used to make the aged chevre.

The goat herd at Dancing Winds Farm now numbers 39, including French Alpine, Oberhasli, Saanen, and African Boer breeds. Mary has a small herd of Cashmere goats for their luxurious wool, and a growing herd of meat goats. Dancing

Winds Farm is now also a destination for people interested in seeing her operation in action or for those who wish to escape to the countryside for a few days. Mary's farmhouse, built in 1856, has been remodeled to include a guest wing that is open as a bed and breakfast retreat. "Guests are welcome to participate in farm activities," says Mary "or to just enjoy the healing energy of the goats and the relaxing country atmosphere."

By treating the goats like family and letting them run free in the pasture to fertilize the fields, eat the weeds, frolic and be goats, Mary has found a balance between small-scale dairy production and a sustainable and healthy product. Dancing Winds Farm is a haven for Mary as well as for those who visit her during the year.

WANG UAB'S ASIAN DELI
Egg Rolls Made Fresh Each Saturday Morning

Pakou Hang was in elementary school when her family started selling vegetables at the St. Paul Farmers' Market. You can still find her at the Market, but she now has a degree from Yale University. Although Pakou and her six siblings are young adults, each pursuing his or her own career path, the enterprise is still very much a family affair. In 2001, the Hang family began to make fresh egg rolls and spring rolls at the St. Paul Farmers' Market. They make the products on-site in a white concession trailer with big red windows.

The Hang family immigrated to the United States in 1976. Upon arriving in this country, Mr. and Mrs. Hang, like many other Hmong parents, soon discovered that their past skills as subsistence farmers did not fit well in a post-industrialized economy like that in the United States. The Hang family, however, worked very hard and worked together, first picking cucumbers in Wisconsin, then renting farmland in St. Paul, and now making eggrolls and spring rolls at the Market.

Throughout their struggles, Mr. and Mrs. Hang were absolutely committed to educating their children and educating them well — first in Catholic schools, then private schools, and now various colleges. The profits from growing and selling vegetables went toward the tuitions of those schools. The second generation of Hangs have studied at Brown, Yale, St. Olaf, and Brandeis — and while they have studied subjects as varied as political science, community health, and art and media, all the children are dedicated to higher education.

"I think it is because the farming we did was such hard work and such a humbling experience for us," says Pakou, "that we became so determined to get our educations." Education has certainly changed the Hang family. The

transition from growing and selling vegetables at the St. Paul Farmers' Market to making and selling egg rolls and spring rolls is a reflection of that change.

The Hangs named the egg roll enterprise after their parents — Wang Uab's Asian Deli. The Deli is committed to sharing knowledge and supporting local farmers and traditionally underrepresented communities. While the Hangs

In addition to the egg roll enterprise, the Hang family continues to actively garden in Rosemount and bring to St. Paul fresh produce including: corn, tomatoes, bok choi, Chinese broccoli, melon, Asian squash, and a popular Hmong bitter green.

Pakou hears others speak of her family's story as "entrepreneurial," but she disagrees. "I'm not sure if our story is so much about being entrepreneurs, as it is about simply surviving — using creativity to survive, using hard work to survive. The land supplied us with numerous academic and life lessons. It would have been a shame if we were not stronger people because of those lessons."

Between vegetable sales and egg rolls or spring rolls made from their father's recipe, the Hang family has quite a summer business. And the St. Paul Farmers'

rely on grocery stores for ingredients in the spring, by mid-summer they make the rounds at the St. Paul Farmers' Market, purchasing lettuce, cilantro, mint, and cucumbers for their spring rolls, and carrots and onions for their egg rolls.

Another example of how much education has changed the Hangs is their new website. Soon you will be able to go to www.hmongfarmers.com to learn more about the Hang family and Wang Uab's Asian Deli. The website will feature what is fresh at the Market, introduce new products being created, and share tasty Asian recipes.

Market is just the place to absorb and direct that business. "The Market is a good place," says Pakou. She has seen subtle changes over the years, more ethnic and socio-economic diversity among the vendors and among the customers and is personally glad that the market is accessible to diverse communities. The evolution of the Market mirrors the evolution of the Hang family

The Hang's is a story of family survival turned business venture; a story about a generation who grew up in vegetable fields, and climbed over Ivy League walls. Find Pakou, her family, and their delicious egg rolls and spring rolls on Saturday and Sunday mornings at the St. Paul Farmers' Market.

JAVA RIVER

Coffee House Hopes to Stir Storefront Revolution

Mary Moore holds up an offering of fresh-brewed gourmet coffee at Java River in downtown Montevideo, Minnesota. Along with husband Patrick, the Moores aim to do far more than introduce the heartland to the luxury of gourmet coffee. Their coffeehouse has a computer — but this is no Internet cafe. It is a cafe where customers can link through a computer kiosk to local farms producing high-quality products.

From a railroad depot in North Redwood, Minnesota, Richard W. Sears once launched a revolution in the way American consumers bought their goods. Patrick and Mary see no reason why they cannot start the next consumer revolution from downtown Montevideo. But the Moores are starting their revolution with a focus on taste — good taste. They also have different aspirations for the Main Streets of rural America than did Sears, the founder of mail order catalogs.

First the matter of taste: the Java River coffeehouse the Moores opened in 1998 brings gourmet brewed coffee to a heartland more familiar with stuff that tastes like it dripped out of the crankcase. "Thank you so much for opening a coffeehouse," local customers repeat mantra-like after their first visit.

Beyond good coffee, Patrick and Mary are hoping to lead a change in the way America buys, and ultimately produces, its agricultural products. The Moores believe that Americans care not only about the quality of the food they buy, but also the manner in which it is produced. "Given the choice," says Patrick, "Americans will buy goods from farms using sustainable agricultural practices because these farms produce food in ways that are beneficial to the environment, and to the Main Streets of the small towns they call home."

Patrick and Mary want to link customers and producers. For starters, they purchase the ingredients to make the delicious soups and sandwiches they serve at Java River from local farmers. To further link customers and producers, they have replaced the Sears mail order catalog with a computer kiosk in the corner of the coffeehouse. At a touch of the finger, patrons have access to sustainable farms in the Montevideo area willing to sell their products directly to consumers. Touch the screen, and the people behind places come to life in pictures and words. Touch the Easy Bean Farm icon and learn how farm owner Mike Jacobs grows fresh, organic produce. Touch the Morning Has Broken Farm icon and learn how farmers Larry and Carolyn Olson raise their cows, lambs, and pigs on pasture to produce tasty meat while reducing erosion in the Minnesota River Valley.

"Social marketing" is what the Moores call this approach of linking customers to producers. They are not alone. A couple of guys by the names of Ben Cohen and Jerry Greenfield brought the same philosophy to the business of selling ice cream. "They set out to make money by marketing their values," says Patrick. The Moores intend to do the same, but they know better than to confuse good intentions with business realities. Patrick has done his research and knows the number one business reality is to know your market. He reports, "Marketing surveys show that twenty-five percent of Americans want to buy sustainable farm produce, but only two to three percent are able to do so."

Of course, it will take more than a kiosk in a coffeehouse to reach that untapped market, so customers can access the same information on their home computers by calling up www.prairiefare.com on the World Wide Web. Farmers featured on the website are hearing from a variety of interested people, according to Patrick. Their hope is that the interest will

manifest itself as an improved market for the products of sustainable farms. "If the market is there," says Audrey Arner, whose farm is featured on the site, "more farmers will adopt sustainable agricultural practices."

It is the kind of change both Audrey and Patrick want to see. Both are organizers for the Land Stewardship Project (LSP), which helped launch this venture and bring the farmers together. LSP also provided the equipment for developing the computer kiosk and the farmers' website. The Moores invested their own funds and sweat equity into developing a coffeehouse in an empty storefront in downtown Montevideo. Even though they are taking the financial risk of operating their own business, the Moores are optimistic, and for good reason. Along with a steady stream of local customers, Java River is attracting to its counter many visitors to Montevideo. "You'd be surprised," says Mary, laughing, "I'm afraid it's kind of a tourist place."

EarthRise Farm
Food with a Farmer's Face on It

Annette and Kay Fernholz, two School Sisters of Notre Dame, and sisters in both the biological and religious sense, returned to their family home in Madison, Minnesota, to begin a dream called EarthRise. EarthRise is a Community Supported Agriculture (CSA) farm, built on four acres of the 240-acre farm where Annette and Kay spent their childhood. "One of our goals is to make a small contribution to growing a new world vision of a more just and humane food supply, where the restoration of community and the art of eating can again be found at the heart of agriculture," says Annette.

"The name, EarthRise, was taken from a statement the first astronauts made as they looked out over the rim of the moon in 1968," says Annette. "They said, 'We have seen the splendor of the Earth rise above the horizon of the moon.'" Annette and Kay feel the name announces a paradigm shift, and as a species with powerful imaginations, we will eventually be transformed by the reality that we have no existence apart from the intelligent, living planet. Their part in realizing this new paradigm is to provide their community with organic, chemical-free food through their CSA.

A CSA farm is one where "subscribers" purchase a "share" in a farming operation. With their purchase, subscribers share in both the rewards and the risks of a growing season. "In our first year, we had seven subscribers," reports Annette. "It was a wait and see year." By their second year, they had twenty subscribers, and thirty the next year. In 2000, the fourth year of the Fernholz sisters' endeavor, fifty subscribers invested in EarthRise Farm. Subscribers, or as some prefer, "partners," receive a weekly share of eight to twenty pounds of food for twenty-two weeks beginning in late May. The sisters grow a variety of food that goes into the shares, including green beans, winter squash, asparagus, broccoli, Swiss chard, spinach, cucumbers, peppers, beets, eggplant, potatoes, tomatoes, cantaloupe, watermelon, pumpkins, eggs, cut flowers, assorted herbs and small surprises. Subscribers also get a newsletter update on garden activities, cooking tips, and folklore relating to the produce. In 2001, full subscribers paid $325, and subscribers for a half share paid $225. A flexible payment plan allows subscribers to pay in installments of $25 or more.

Annette and Kay encourage members to take part in the garden. "This is not 'our' garden," says Kay. "It is 'their' (the partners) garden." They invite all participants to help tend the garden and watch the splendor of the earth as it follows nature's cycles. They also extend the welcome to non-members. Annette and Kay regularly facilitate community gatherings, celebrations, and events at their farm. One example is the annual Environmental Sabbath prayer service, which includes activities to celebrate the earth. At the center of the farm is a spiral Meditation Path that symbolically represents the earth's fifteen billion year story. "On the Environmental Sabbath, people gather here to reflect and pray for guidance through these challenging times of earth healing," says Annette.

is growing every year. "Our most serious complaint from shareholders," Kay says, "is that we put too much food in their shares." Every year sees increased community participation and awareness of EarthRise Farm and its values. And every year, there is an increase in community members willing to hope, take a leap of faith, and join EarthRise Farm to access, as the sisters say, "food with a farmer's face on it." In the words of the founder of their order of sisters, Mother Theresa Gerhardinger, "All the works of God proceed slowly and in pain; but then, their roots are the sturdier and their flowering the lovelier."

Annette and Kay have great visions and plans for their farm. Currently, they host seasonal interns who live and work at EarthRise. The sisters also bring "garden angels" — children and high school students — to their garden to help during the summer. In the future, they hope to sponsor earth literacy classes.

"In a market economy," Annette says, "we vote with our dollars." With this in mind, the sisters want EarthRise Farm to provide families and communities the opportunity to cast a vote for the type of food system, the type of land use, and ultimately, the type of community they want each time they sit down at the dinner table. The Fernholz sisters "dare" the community to "join them" in revitalizing and restoring the infrastructure of rural America.

The positive response to their diverse garden amidst fields of corn and soybeans

MINNESOTA CERTIFIED PORK

Cooperative Formed by States' Hog Producers

Whenever Larry Liepold goes into a grocery store, he makes a beeline to the meat counter to see what people are buying. Larry is a pork producer from Okabena, Minnesota, and has served as president of the Minnesota Pork Producers Association (MPPA). In the summer of 2001, Larry and four other farm families had a deeply personal interest in seeing how pork was selling at Kowalski's Market in Woodbury, Minnesota. The farmers ventured to the store to introduce pork raised and processed through Minnesota Certified Pork — a new cooperative they formed to market pork that is certified to meet high production and quality standards.

The pork from the cooperative was the first product to go through Minnesota Certified, a third-party certification program run by the University of Minnesota and Minnesota Department of Agriculture (MDA). The program is known as MinnCERT. The voluntary program allows farmers to develop production standards that appeal to consumer demands for product quality and animal care, says Dave Starner, a Hoffman, Minnesota hog producer who is a former MPPA president. The University and MDA ensure standards are met.

Dave Starner started the project in 1998 when pork prices dropped to a record low for farmers. He helped develop the program's model with Thomas Blaha, professor of Veterinary Medicine at the University, and Jerry Shurson, professor of Animal Science. The pork is sold at Kowalski's stores in Woodbury, White Bear Lake, Inver Grove Heights and St. Paul. It also will be distributed through SuperValu to two grocery chains.

Boyd Oase, meat manager for Kowalski's, says there seems to be good consumer response to Minnesota Certified Pork. It will take some time to accumulate sales figures to see just how good that consumer response is. The idea behind selling pork that is seen as higher quality than commodity cuts appeals to Kowalski's because the market serves a clientele that does not mind paying more for food if it is a good value. Kowalski's also wants to shore up sales of pork, which had slipped in comparison with beef and poultry. "My expectation is it will improve our sales for pork," Boyd says. "Any area where we can get better shelf movement is good for us."

"The Cooperative's hogs are processed at Swift and Company's plant in Worthington, Minnesota, to make it easier for consumers and others to trace the meat's origins and to maintain high processing standards," Dave says. The five farmers will supply 1100 hogs a week to the Cooperative. If the concept is successful, other farmers will be invited to join the Cooperative and buy stock, he says. The hope is there will be so much demand for certified pork that more processors and grocery chains will come on-line.

In addition to Larry and Dave, other farmers in the Cooperative include Jim Quackenbush of Chokio, David and Karen Richter of Montgomery, and John Vaubel of Mapleton. Their herd sizes vary from 125 to 2000 sows. The Richters and other Cooperative members say they wanted to move away from the uncertainties of the commodity pork market while meeting consumer demands for quality and the ability to trace animals back to the farm. "It seemed like a progressive move for our operation," Karen Richter says. "The industry is changing; the average consumer is changing. They want to know where their food is produced." Karen believes that many people want to help family farmers, but do not know how. The Cooperative makes putting more money in farmers' pockets as easy as going to the grocery store.

The Richters say the production guidelines are already being met by many producers — the only difference is the University and MDA are assuring standards are met. After looking at pork with the MinnCERT label in the meat case, Larry Liepold cannot help but smile.

CHAPTER THREE
Product Innovations

When these Minnesota business people strive for innovation in a product, their imaginations spill over into all elements of their enterprise. Read of chocolate buttermilk, organic cotton jackets, or hazel oil, and you will also learn of the creative processes behind these products. A special commitment to freshness, family-first management styles, soil-saving techniques, and cooperative business structures are as much "product" as they are "process" in these stories.

Innovation as a contagion spreads throughout these businesses and creates what one man tags "enlightened capitalism." Part of the success of these small-scale ventures is also their creative no-waste practices. When we read of junk mail as hog bedding or rag rugs woven from scraps, we might look around our own homes and imagine using 'waste' differently. If creativity begins with the idea of a product, and spreads into innovative business processes, might it also infuse itself into the lifestyles of the customers themselves?

BADGERSETT RESEARCH CORPORATION
Agriculture Gone Nuts

Badgersett Research Farm looks unlike any farm in the region. On this 160 acres of rolling farmland in Fillmore County, there are neither rows of corn and soybeans, nor rows of carrots, tomatoes, and cucumbers. What you will see are rows of hazel bushes and chestnut trees. This is what Philip Rutter, founder of Badgersett Research Corporation, calls "woody agriculture." Philip has a vision. He would like to see some of the Midwest's corn and soybean fields replaced with highly domesticated, food-producing, woody plants. This woody agriculture, he believes, will not only provide environmental benefits, but will also be profitable to the region's farmers.

In the early 1970s, when Philip was studying zoology at the University of Minnesota, he fell in love with southeast Minnesota and built a small log home, tucked in the woods. Deeply interested in evolution and ecology, Philip investigated his new farm's geological history. An old land survey showed one hill on his farm had as much as eighteen inches of topsoil in 1950. In 1975, nowhere on that hill was the topsoil deeper than six inches. "This is some of the best agricultural soil in the world," explains Philip, "but it's fragile. It got here as dust during the glacial period and it washes away easily."

Philip also discovered the area was once oak-hazel savanna. "The hazel roots successfully competed with sod and the tops withstood fire, but they were wiped out by cows and plows," explains Philip. Convinced woody agriculture would keep the topsoil on his rolling hills intact, Philip began breeding hazels and chestnuts. Though he had completed the coursework for a Ph.D., rather than finishing it, Philip picked up a Master's degree and started Badgersett, a British term meaning "badger's home."

For the past twenty-five years, Philip and his family have been in the plant breeding business. In their solar earth-sheltered greenhouse, they have crossed local hazelnut and chestnut varieties with species from around the world to develop plant lines that are disease-resistant and suited to northern climates. Over 10,000 hazelnut and chestnut plants have been evaluated at Badgersett, and there are 120,000 more in the testing phase. "Breeding woody plants requires a long time commitment" Philip explains, "but the payoff is that we now have plant lines that are healthy, hardy, and produce nuts at a commercial scale."

Of the two woody perennials, hazelnuts are best suited for Minnesota because they are native, grow quickly with abundant yields, and resist disease and harsh weather. "These hybrid hazels are environmentally unstoppable here," Philip explains. "There's nothing the weather can do to even challenge them. They survive 40-below-zero temperatures untouched." An abundance of bug-eating frogs, birds, and predatory insects eliminate the need for pesticides at Badgersett. A few tall, dead trees placed throughout the groves attract hawks, which keep mice and squirrels away. Recently, Philip began experimenting with geese to "mow" the grass strips between the rows of bushes and trees.

Badgersett hazel bushes grow nine- to fourteen-feet high in sun or part shade, can bear nuts when three- to five-years old, and withstand both dry and wet conditions, once established. Deep, spreading roots tolerate both heavy clay and sandy soils. The bushes produce clusters of nuts — about three pounds per year on the better plants — adding up to between one and four thousand pounds per acre annually. Philip remarks, "Our record is eight pounds on a bush, and every time we ask plants to do something

more for us, we discover they can. The plants grow several times faster than we thought they could."

Philip is not alone in his interest in making hazels a viable crop for farmers in the Midwest. Other researchers, organizations and individuals have demonstrated their support by partnering with Badgersett on projects, providing financial support, or purchasing plants. The National Arbor Day Foundation, for example, planted several acres of Badgersett hazels and chestnuts in front of their conference center in Nebraska. They are using these plants for research and demonstration purposes, and in 2001 harvested their first ton of nuts — 3500 pounds, actually.

A partnership with researchers at the University of Nebraska has led to breakthroughs in reproducing hazel plants more quickly. The best plant lines are being cloned and tested. The goal is hazel plants that are uniform in size and productivity. The benefit of this uniformity is that hazel bushes can then be harvested with a machine that drives much like a combine.

The Experiment in Rural Cooperation, one of the University of Minnesota's Regional Sustainable Development Partnerships, is working with Badgersett to develop a business plan and a "how to" guide for raising hazels. It also is helping to support research that will enable other farmers in the area to successfully grow hazels. Other support has come from the Agricultural Utilization and Research Institute and the Minnesota Department of Agriculture's Energy and Sustainable Agriculture Program. Badgersett is also cooperating with forty farmers from around the country, each raising two or more acres of hazelnuts, to form a growers group to collaborate on value-added products and marketing.

Hazelnut markets are promising around the globe. Also known as filberts, hazels are popular for eating shelled, in cooking, and in gourmet foods such as Italian-made Nutella, a blend of hazelnuts and chocolate. Scandinavians are known for their hazelnut pastries, which were once part of the American-Scandinavian cuisine until hazelnuts became scarce. The aromatic, flavorful oil is used in coffee, honey, and even candles. Because of their high oil content, "anything you can do with soybeans, you can do with hazels," Philip says. The 70-percent monounsaturated oil (the healthiest kind) is popular with Europeans, who use it like olive oil. In fact, Badger Oil in Wisconsin "buys hazels from Turkey, presses them here, and sells the oil to France," explains Philip. The company recently pressed a test batch of Badgersett hazels, which could open another market.

Chestnuts are more challenging. "This is the coldest, driest place in the world where anybody tries to seriously breed chestnuts," explains Philip. Despite the challenges, he is convinced that developing the right

chestnut hybrids for the Midwest will yield a high-value crop that could also serve as windbreaks. Badgersett chestnuts grow fast and yield high-starch, high-protein, low-oil nuts with potential uses similar to corn. Besides the old-fashioned "roasting on an open fire" treatment, chestnuts are candied in Europe and Japan. The nuts are also ground for bread, pasta, stuffing, and animal feed. "Not only do the trees produce food," says Philip, "but their timber is rot-resistant, lighter than oak, splits easily and is stable when dry, making it suitable for shingles and other products."

Badgersett sells its hazel and chestnuts seedlings over the Internet at www.badgersett.com. In 2001, seedlings cost from two to seven dollars apiece. After studying the proper methods to dry and store hazelnuts and chestnuts for packaging and distribution, Badgersett now sells a limited quantity of nuts over the Internet. "We are now becoming a mainstream enterprise, with the intention of making a profit," says Philip, who is now selling Badgersett Research Corporation stock through a private offering. And with the growing interest in hazelnuts as an alternative Midwestern crop, Philip is hoping that farmers in the region will also find profits in hazelnuts.

WILDROSE FARM
Stitching Full Circle

Chuck and Karen Knierim like to make lunch for their employees at Wildrose Farm in Breezy Point, Minnesota. Chuck, a former logger, and Karen, a custom seamstress turned clothing designer, believe that a commitment to a healthier planet involves making a commitment to their employees. Besides daily lunch, which may include eggs from the Knierim's flock of hens, organic produce from the farm's garden, or milk from the farm's goat herd, Wildrose employees have a flexible work-schedule, deep discounts on the company's products, and a "sew your own day." For the latter, Chuck and Karen provide the equipment and the organic fabric necessary for employees to make their own clothing.

"All the women who work here have their own families. We let them set the schedules to keep us pro-family," Karen says. "A child who is ill comes first, and a doctor's appointment assumes priority over a rigid production time table." Chuck and Karen take the same responsible approach to their customers. Wildrose Farm makes organic cotton clothing. Because organic cotton is not treated with formaldehyde or chlorine as is regular cotton, organic cotton fabric does not cause skin irritation or allergic reactions. Organic cotton — the Knierims only use American grown — is also softer and more supple, according to Chuck. Wildrose Farm sells its goods through the Internet at www.wildrosefarm.com, at the Wildrose Organics store in Pequot Lakes, Minnesota, and nationally through a Massachusetts wholesale marketer.

A manufacturer's responsibility does not start with the customer or even the employees, as far as Chuck and Karen are concerned. It starts with the company's suppliers. "We thoroughly check out all suppliers to see if they really are making organic products and if their items are truly natural," Chuck says. Chuck and Karen continue to educate consumers who want high-quality, chemical-free products about the nature of cotton agriculture. "The claim of 'organic' for cotton is unusual," explains Chuck. "Few people are aware, for example, that conventional cotton is grown on three percent of American agricultural land, but uses twenty five percent of the nation's agricultural chemicals."

The organic cotton products made by the Knierims and their staff include dresses, skirts, jackets, jumpers, pants, shirts, coats, and quilts. They also have a line of organic cotton T-shirts on which they can custom screen, block print, hand paint, dye, or batik dye images or logos. In fact, they recently created a T-shirt for the Central Chapter of the Sustainable Farming Association of Minnesota.

The concept of full-circle responsibility has taken the Knierims down some interesting paths as a business. In 1999, Wildrose Farm received the Governor's Award for Excellence in Waste and Pollution Prevention. The genesis of the award was based, in part, on a desire to save the beautiful scraps of cloth left over after

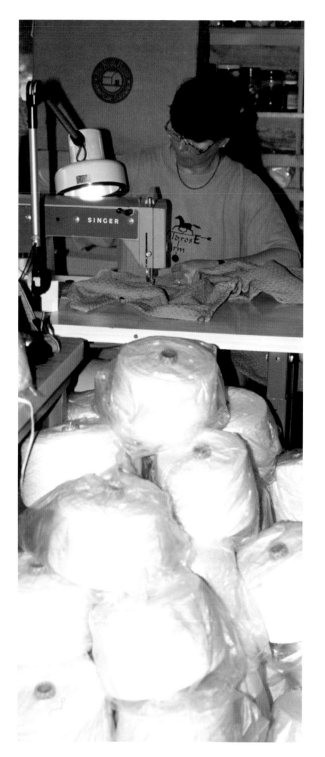

cutting out patterns. "We didn't want to throw anything away because we had such great stuff (organic cotton)" Chuck explains. "A lot of people work hard, including the farmers who grow it, to produce a quality product. We wanted to show respect for their work by not throwing it away."

With that in mind, Karen applied for, and received, a grant from the Minnesota Office of Environmental Assistance. The plan was to reclaim 100 percent of the waste fabric. With $20,417 in grant funds, Wildrose Farm devised a system for manufacturing cotton rugs from the fabric scraps. Instead of moldering in a landfill, the scraps, as rugs, now grace and warm the floors of appreciative customers. Likewise, waste cotton, too small to be woven into rugs, is turned into a high-quality acid-free paper desired by artists for watercolor painting. Unlike conventional paper manufacturing, no toxic wastes are created when the Wildrose cotton paper is made.

In addition to nourishing Wildrose Farm employees with delicious, healthy lunches, Chuck also works to nourish his land. He is sustainably managing the woods on their twenty-two acre farmstead, part of which is established as a Certified Tree Farm. Chuck carefully selects pine trees from his woods to use as lumber in the new buildings needed to expand Wildrose's clothing enterprise. Scrap wood is harvested for firewood that fuels an efficient, central, hot water heating system for all the buildings on the farm. Chuck's appreciation of the elegant pine lumber of his farm is similar to his partiality towards organically produced cotton fabric. As an expression of that appreciation, he created a line of unique hand-decorated pine boxes made from Wildrose Farm lumber.

Chuck and Karen envision their company as part of an economy that has loops of responsibility beyond the company's bottom line. That economy will be one that cares as much for the vendors and employees of a company as it does for the company's owners and its profits. It will be an economy that nurtures equally those resources in the company's backyard and those on other continents. And this "enlightened capitalism," as Chuck calls it, will be profitable for all concerned.

SNO PAC FOODS
Organic for Nearly Sixty Years

Pete Gengler is happy that his family got into the organic food business early. Sno Pac, the first grower/processor of frozen organic vegetables, was founded in 1943 in Caledonia, Minnesota. It is now in its third generation of ownership and has evolved into a world class processor of organic fruit and vegetable products. Pete's mother, Darlene, is the last of the second generation, working in the office in Accounts Payable. The third generation includes Pete, president; Nick Gengler, the production manager; and Joan Gengler, their sister, who lives on the farm and works in the office. Family involvement has been a cornerstone of day-to-day operations since the company was founded.

Unlike many farmers, the Genglers don't worry much about crop prices. "We can stay in business because we create our own market by growing, processing, and packaging our products and being able to store them," says Pete. Sno Pac has about fifteen percent of the nation's frozen organic food market. The Organic Trade Association, amongst others, expects the demand for frozen organics to continue to grow. Sno Pac's biggest competitor is Cascadian Farms in Washington State, which was recently purchased by General Mills.

Everything the Genglers do today connects with something in the family's past. In the early 1900s, Pete's great-grandfather, John Peter Gengler, founded the Gengler Lumber Company. In the 1920s, John built a pond at the lumber mill site and started a side business of harvesting ice from the pond, packing the ice blocks in sawdust from the mill, storing them in an ice box, and shipping them south in the summer months.

When refrigeration became available, Leonard Nicholas, Pete's entrepreneurial grandfather, started Caledonia Cold Storage to accommodate the family's slaughter and butcher operation on its farm. Townspeople and local farmers rented freezer space from the Gengler's locker plant to store their food. In the 1930s, the family also began growing organic fruits and vegetables and storing them in the lockers. During World War II, Leonard Nicholas packaged the frozen food under the Sno Pac label, and a niche market of frozen organic products was created.

From the beginning, the Gengler family farmed organically, using natural fertilizers and practicing soil conservation methods. When chemicals were introduced to the farming community, the Genglers were contacted by people from around the country who wanted organic products. Now the family grows wheat and alfalfa for crop rotation and plows in the residue to fertilize the organic fields. "We don't have too much of an insect issue with organic. The big issue is the weed pressure," according to Pete.

The Sno Pac product line now includes fruits and vegetables. Blueberries, strawberries, chopped spinach, golden corn, green peas, cranberries, cut green beans and sweet beans are all among the staple line. The company has also begun marketing newer products like Southern Style Hash Browns and Soycoutash (a mixture of vegetable soy, red peppers and corn). In addition, Pete has introduced organic edamame to the U.S. market. Edamame, meaning "beans on branches," are soybeans picked before they reach maturity, resulting in a sweeter flavor. Commonly found in Japanese restaurants as appetizers, and served in the pod, edamame were once imported from Japan and Taiwan and were available only through Asian grocers. "For ten years or more, Sno Pac has been developing the best variety and processing procedures for edamame in the U.S.," Pete states. And while edamame has been a snack food in Japan for centuries, it only recently has caught on in the U.S.

Sno Pac products are truly "fresh frozen." Once produce is harvested and brought from the field to the processing plant, it takes seven to ten minutes for it to be placed in a freezer. From the truck, smaller items like peas are put through a shaker — a machine that shakes off waste like sticks and leaves. A conveyor belt transfers the produce to a bin for washing. The washed produce is moved to a blanching machine where it is boiled at 205° Fahrenheit for two minutes.

After blanching, the product moves into a computer-calibrated separator that removes smaller waste and unusable produce, and sorts produce by certain sizes, shapes, and colors automatically. Depending on quality and volume, three to five employees will also manually sift through the produce before it is transferred to the freezer. The final produce is transferred into the freezer storage area, which is approximately fifty feet away.

Sno Pac recently switched to frozen produce bags instead of their traditional cartons due to a change in consumer preference. "We're trying to stay competitive," Pete says. Sno Pac also sells to food manufacturers that combine its produce in recipes for other products. Its vegetables are used in the Amy's Kitchen brand, ShariAnn's soups, and Gerber's baby foods (under the Tender Harvest label). Sno Pac label products are distributed nationally to colleges, cafeterias, health food stores, buying clubs and retail stores. The retail market contributes the most to Sno Pac's profit margins.

Sno Pac is enjoying a twenty percent annual increase in growth. Despite the high growth-rate and astonishing success of Sno Pac foods, Pete admits that the family continues to invest hard work in order to grow their company. "Every day is a challenge for us," says Pete. "We have to deal with the weather, equipment breakdowns, personnel issues and increasing competition in the organic food industry." But in the end, Pete feels gratified that he contributes to the supply of healthy foods for American tables.

PET CARE SYSTEMS, INCORPORATED

The Difference is in the Wheat

"In the year 2000, cats surpassed dogs as Americans' most favorite pet!" exclaims Mark Hughes. "There are at least seventy million cats registered as pets in the United States." Mark cares about these statistics because he and his parents, Vonnie and Mike Hughes, cater to cats — or rather, cat owners. In 1994, the Hughes started Pet Care Systems and launched one of the most successful alternative pet care products in the United States — Swheat Scoop. Swheat Scoop is a cat litter made from wheat that offers an effective, safe, and biodegradable alternative to clay-based litters.

"That's the unique thing about our business – none of us would be here without each other. I wouldn't be here without my mom and dad and they wouldn't be here without me," says Mark. Mike, Mark's dad, is the president of the company, Vonnie is the office manager, and Mark is the sales and marketing director. The other family members in the office are the Hughes' cats! "My parents have three cats that come into the office on Mondays, Wednesdays and Fridays," says Mark. "They are the official tester cats – Scoop, Tinker and Lady."

As Mark tells the story, a farmer in Fergus Falls hated the odor from his cats' litter box. One day, he was looking out at his wheat fields and had an idea. He ground up some of his wheat, put it in the litter box, and it solved the odor problem! The farmer brought his idea to a local marketing firm in Fergus Falls where Mark was introduced to the product. It was clear the product had great potential; the problem was finding someone to invest in the idea. Excited by the opportunity, Mark called his parents and asked if they would consider investing in a new product. "My parents had always had cats, so they were familiar with the odor," Mark explains. "When they tried it, they thought it was the best litter that they had ever used." And so the family business was started.

Marketing savvy has been a cornerstone of Pet Care Systems success. The company sells three main product lines: Swheat Scoop, City Litter and Wheat and Easy. The curious thing is that they are all exactly the same – just targeted for different markets. Mark sells Swheat Scoop, their longest running and biggest selling line, to Petsmart, larger Target stores, and Petco stores. City Litter is distributed to grocery stores and mass market accounts like WalMart. Wheat and Easy is sold to veterinarians and smaller food markets.

Mark understands that people have different buying habits. Some feel that they are buying a better product if they buy from a pet store. Others want the convenience of picking up pet products at the grocery store. Still others trust their veterinarian to carry the best product. "Local pet stores don't want to carry the same brand as the large grocers and retail stores because they cannot compete," explains Mark. "The larger businesses will always be able to buy the product at a cheaper rate simply because of the volumes they buy."

In their first year, Pet Care Systems sold nearly $50,000 worth of cat litter. Now the company goes through more than twice that amount in a single month. This amount of production benefits local wheat farmers who value this new market. Producers often directly contact Pet Care Systems with bins full of low-protein, low-weight wheat that they cannot sell elsewhere. The Hughes specifically buy only non-food grade wheat so as to create a market for a product that often goes to waste.

To the farmers' benefit, the family is ambitious about that market. When they built their processing plant in Detroit Lakes, now the company's headquarters, they built with expansion in mind. The plant handles eight to ten truckloads of wheat a month, and could produce up to 1000 truckloads of finished product a year.

Why are they so optimistic? Two reasons. First, the market for environmentally-sound products is growing, especially overseas. According to Mark, Pet Care Systems gets a lot of calls from countries around the world that have smaller landfills than those in the United States. "Clay litters are not biodegradable and just take up space," Mark says. "Our litter is 100 percent biodegradable and can be flushed down the toilet. In Europe they are having trouble with people flushing the clay-based litters and it is winding up on their riverbanks. Some countries are even thinking of outlawing the disposal of clay-based litters in the garbage."

Second, there is growing concern that silica dust, found in clay-based litters, may play a role in cat and human respiratory problems. A study released in July of 2001 connected silica dusts directly with respiratory diseases in tested cats. People who use clay-based litters know that when they fill the litter boxes, a cloud of noxious dust is kicked up. Wheat-based litters do not carry these associated risks. Mark is anxious to see the study hit the major news networks. "Think about it," he says, "one in three households has a cat. If this story goes public, it will be huge."

It is a combination of hard work, a good product, and consumers' interest in healthier, more environmentally-friendly goods that has made Pet Care Systems a success. And it is the Hughes' commitment to the local economy that has made theirs an outstanding rural business.

PRODUCT INNOVATIONS

MOM'S DAIRY

Minnesota Organic Milk — The Cream Rises to the Top

After years of being on the shelves of numerous Twin Cities food cooperatives and grocery stores, the bright blue and green half-gallon cartons of MOM's — that stands for Minnesota Organic Milk — are now familiar to thousands of quality-conscious shoppers.

The Hartmans — Mike, Diane, and Mike's brother Roger — are the family behind this successful organic dairy. "When we were planning the dairy in the early 1990s, we had fifty-two farms lined up to go," Mike recalls, "but every way we figured, it didn't work financially." The point of establishing a farmer-owned creamery was to capture the processing and marketing profits for the farmer owners. When it was clear that the large creamery idea would not fly, the Hartmans decided to build a smaller version on their own farm. They bought used, small equipment sized to their thirty-five cow herd.

Mike is now an advocate of on-farm dairy processing. He and his family operate an exclusively organic dairy processing plant in Minnesota. "Small on-farm creameries can help rejuvenate the countryside," he says. "They can make small dairies like ours profitable, which will create economic opportunities in towns. And urban people will be drawn back to the rural areas."

The vehicle for this economic renaissance is a milk processing room not much larger than a typical living room. It is filled — not jammed — with dairy processing equipment that Mike has located from as far and wide as Wyoming and Pennsylvania. What Mike found allows MOM's to bottle two kinds of milk (skim and two percent), make a range of flavored ice creams, make butter, and most recently, bottle chocolate buttermilk. "Our creamery is what I call diversity within diversity," Mike says.

The diversity and flexibility of the creamery reflect the diversity of the Hartman farm. In addition to the dairy, the farm has pigs, chickens, and a variety of crops. The Hartmans take advantage of natural connections that an industrial-style farm would avoid in the name of efficiency. "The sows act as protection from predators for the chickens," Mike says, "and a portion of the rinse water from the creamery, rich with milk solids, is fed to the pigs."

Mike's philosophy is that there is no such thing as waste on a farm. The Hartmans even throw their junk mail to the hogs. "The old story is that hogs like to spend one-third of their time sleeping, one-third of their time eating and one-third of their time in destructive activity," Mike says. "They shred all that paper, mix it in with the bedding and manure, and it makes a good carbon source for the fields."

The idea that well-run farms have no waste products has served MOM's customers well. MOM's has kept their prices competitive. "We've learned how to operate more efficiently. That's where we've been able to generate our wealth," Mike explains. Roger likes to joke that milk is itself a waste product. "In the old days, farmers would separate the milk from the cream," he says. "The only thing they hauled to town was the cream; they fed the milk to the pigs." At MOM's, the milk is the cake, and the products from the cream — vanilla, chocolate chip molasses, and chocolate ice cream, and butter — are the frosting. "Vanilla out sells the flavored ice creams four or five to one," Mike says. "People would rather add their own toppings."

Roger explains a new initiative that makes use of another underutilized product. "There is a point — it happens all of a sudden — when the buttermilk separates from the butter," he says. In the past, the buttermilk would have gone to the pigs or the chickens. Recently, the Hartmans have been adding organic chocolate syrup to the uncultured buttermilk. "We've been letting people taste it, and they keep coming back for more," says Roger. The Hartmans are waiting until their glass-bottling and washing operation is finished before marketing the buttermilk. The glass-bottling project is pure MOM's in style. Mike and Roger located a used glass-bottling machine and brought it home. Now, they are studying how it operates, cleaning it, and getting it ready to run.

As in any business, customers and marketing are vital. MOM's marketing program is as diverse as the rest of the farm. They sell to food cooperatives, grocers, and a farmer-owned marketing cooperative. They also sell to consumer-managed buying clubs. Although most of their markets are in Minneapolis and St. Paul, they have a home delivery route in the nearby town of New Ulm.

Part of MOM's customer service program has been to hold prices steady. Another part is a product guarantee. "If our milk stays on the shelf beyond the expiration date, we bring it back home and feed it to the pigs," Mike says. MOM's dates their cartons for a three-week shelf life. Roger figures they could get six weeks if they were able to control handling of the milk themselves. "We like to handle the distribution so that we know the milk has been properly refrigerated when it reaches the store cooler," Roger says. "After that, there are so many things that can happen, like a cooler not working or a customer putting the milk in a hot car, that we're better off with a three week expiration."

Roger, who does a lot of MOM's marketing, says people ask him if he drinks his own milk. The answer is yes and no. "I drink the milk from the creamery to test it," he says, "but I prefer milk straight from the bulk tank. It's really delicious."

MOM's cannot sell milk straight from the bulk tank, so their goal is to get certified organic dairy products to their customers that tastes as close to the sweet, fresh taste of "straight-from-the-bulk-tank" as processing rules allow. That includes lower pasteurization temperatures, minimal agitation, no homogenization of bottled milk, and careful handling of the finished product. The final result is happy customers who keep buying MOM's products.

CHAPTER FOUR
Harvesting Nature

Products harvested from nature come directly from the magic of photosynthesis. These stories illustrate how the sun's energy is harvested as quality timber, maple syrup, or glazes and clay for pottery. Yet careful attention to the community's use of our sun's rays shows up here as well. These ventures also raise children among beautiful trees or in the potter's home, and teach traditional culture in the sugar bush.

When we come this close to nature, we cannot help but speak of art. Here you will read of the artistry of a hand-made chair or hand-thrown pot. And keep your reading eyes peeled for solar streams. See how sunshine is sold in jars of jam. Not that long ago in these hills and valleys of Minnesota, nature was the basis for most products created for home use or sold in the general store. These stories may take you back to those days while they open possibilities for the harvesting of nature in modern day life.

SNOWY PINES REFORESTATION
Multigenerational Wealth

"Planting trees is like sending a message in a bottle," says Greg Nolan. "Forestry takes time. Think of trees as living machines — they produce clean air, clean water, timber, habitat, recreational opportunities, and hope for future generations." Greg and his wife, Marcia Rapitz, have a passion for trees. This passion led to the creation of Snowy Pines Reforestation, a service-oriented forestry business committed to sustainable forestry and reforestation near Browerville, Minnesota.

Snowy Pines is grounded in the principles of providing quality services and quality timber. Greg and Marcia have over forty-five years of forestry experience between them. Their business includes tree planting, cone and acorn collection, conifer release, timber stand improvement and harvest, superior seed culturing, trail construction, prescribed burning, maple syrup production, Christmas tree shaping, sawmill operation, lumber and log grading, forestry consulting, and selling firewood.

Reforestation work is the foundation of their business and accounts for sixty to eighty percent of their income. "Some years, we plant more than a quarter-million trees," says Greg. Greg and Marcia provide services that enhance the natural environment and create meaningful, rewarding work for their family and friends. "This work is rewarding not only because it lets us be outdoors

and keep in good shape, but it also lets us protect a resource we truly love," explains Marcia.

In addition to their reforestation work, the business includes a sawmill that processes 60,000 to 70,000 board feet of lumber each year. While small in comparison to other sawmills in the state, Snowy Pines strives for top quality lumber. Every particle of wood that goes through the sawmill is used — the sawdust for trails or given away to horse farmers, and the scraps for firewood. The sawmill gives the family another source of income and complements their forest management business. Greg and Marcia carefully manage the wood resources on their own land. Greg explains that selective logging, when done right, enhances natural regeneration of the forest.

Beyond their own livelihood, Greg and Marcia see a great potential for forestry in their community — a way to take care of resources and generate economic development. "We can build great forests in Todd County," says Greg, "but it will take foresight and management with an eye towards sustainability." According to Greg, the cycle has been set back by people "mining" the forest instead of managing it. "The initial loggers of Todd County's pine and hardwood forests basically clear-cut the timber, took the money, and ran," explains Greg.

With 135,000 acres of forests remaining in Todd County, Greg and others would like to see these lands managed sustainably, and the wood used to create new jobs and wealth. Greg has been a driving force behind the fledgling Headwaters Forestry Cooperative. This member-controlled cooperative is organized to improve the conditions of local forests, and the relationships people have with them, by adding value to the forest products, promoting economic development, and improving water quality in the Mississippi Headwaters region.

Greg uses his land as an example. When he and Marcia bought their land a couple of decades ago, a state forester estimated they owned 20,000 board feet of white pine on three acres of the land. They could have cleared that land and taken a quick profit. Instead, they have managed the forest, made a living from it, and through careful selection of the trees they cut, now have 65,000 board feet of lumber on that same three acres.

The Headwaters Forestry Cooperative is following the international standards developed through the Forest Stewardship Council (FSC) and striving to have its products certified and labeled as SmartWood. SmartWood brings foresters, manufacturers, conservationists and consumers together to improve forest management. The SmartWood program requires chain-of-custody certification, thus assuring buyers that their wood was harvested in a sustainable manner. SmartWood certification is based on the idea that when managed effectively, timber production can maintain the long-term viability of commercial forests, protect the environment, and provide economic benefits to the local community.

"The scope of the co-op is broad," says Greg, "and will include cooperative marketing strategies and value-added products such as flooring, solid wood sheathing, pine logs, rafters, firewood, and even hunting cabins." Greg's sawmill has recently become SmartWood certified. Greg would like to see the co-op develop a team of carpenters who know how to work with native materials, as well as a team of wood floor installers. He would also love to see local wood used to create high quality, affordable housing in Todd County.

Greg and Marcia's commitment to reforestation has also involved them in community projects. Greg is a key organizer of the Long Prairie River Stewardship Project. The project focuses on planting trees along the river to increase water quality, wildlife, and the river's natural beauty for the community. In a six-year span, the project planted over 65,000 trees on approximately twelve miles of river frontage, encompassing the land of forty different owners. Greg remarks, "The citizens of this community are the most powerful tool we have to make positive changes on the landscape."

The same values that drive their business and community organizing efforts are apparent in Greg and Marcia's lifestyle. They have raised their children, Moriah, Cheyenne, Forest, and Senora on forty acres of woodlands. Their meandering driveway winds through a cathedral of white pine up to their solar-powered home. The house was designed to make maximum use of the sun as a power source and was built primarily from wood harvested and milled from their own land. Not surprisingly, Marcia grows most of the food they eat on a one-acre organic garden.

Greg and Marcia have built their business on three basic building blocks: having respect for the next generation, using individual and community intelligence in making business decisions, and making a secure community. Greg says, "As a community, I want to write sentences to the people in the twenty-first century with projects that say 'We gave thanks for the wealth that we have by investing in the natural systems around us, where all wealth starts.' This is a kind of multigenerational wealth. More than anything else, I want the people who come after we're gone to look at us as intelligent people who could work together, because we are."

MINNESOTA WILD

A Visit to Grandma's Kitchen

Jay Erckenbrack has powerful memories of visiting his grandparents as a child. "Both my grandmothers made tremendous breads and rolls. I remember the fresh hot bread coming out of the oven, putting homemade jelly on it, and eating it warm," says Jay, now owner of Minnesota Wild, in McGregor, Minnesota. "Not a bad way to start a day!"

That statement is as pure Minnesota-speak as the products of Minnesota Wild are pure Minnesotan. Jay's driving passion for more than a decade has been to evoke memories of Grandma's for his customers through his line of fruit jams and syrups. In 1994, Jay brought Grandpa into the picture; he started a winery. "I have this picture of Grandma in the kitchen making jelly, and Grandpa in the basement making wine," he remarks.

When Jay and Lori Gordon, Minnesota Wild's general manager, sat down a dozen years ago to imagine what products could result from a trip to grandma and grandpa's house, the list was long. It took them nearly six years to get around to the winery, and they are still spinning out new products that Jay's grandparents, feeling inventive and perhaps a bit whimsical, might have turned out. The company recently introduced blueberry salsa. "The underlying flavor is salsa, but the blueberry really comes through," says Jay.

Jay and Lori worked in the Minnesota paddy rice industry before launching Minnesota Wild. When they left, they were interested in marketing lake and stream wild rice. It was clear, however, that nobody could make much of a living selling one-pound bags of rice. It was not a great leap for them to move from hand-gathered wild rice to hand-gathered wild fruits. Although Minnesota Wild has branched out into non-food products, fruits remain central to the business. Each year, they process tons of wild chokecherries,

blackberries, black currants, high bush cranberries, Juneberries, blueberries, pincherries, plums, grapes, and raspberries.

Anishinaabe people from the Leech Lake and White Earth Reservations play a critical role in the business. They gather nearly half the wild fruit Minnesota Wild uses in its products. "We have a buying program at Leech Lake Reservation," Jay explains. "We'll tell them we want 5000 pounds of chokecherries, 5000 pounds of blueberries, and 2000 pounds of plums. They put a list out around the reservation and people bring the fruit to the fisheries building at Cass Lake where they are paid when they drop it off." The fruit is put in a freezer there until Minnesota Wild staff pick it up.

Since growing grapes in northern Minnesota would have been a dicey proposition, Minnesota Wild's wines are crafted from other fruits. There are fourteen different wines with two new ones in the making. The wines are made by blending fruit wine with honey wine, or mead. Jay likes using mead because Minnesota apiaries produce an abundance of high quality honey.

Blending honey and fruit wines, however, is challenging for the winemaker. "With honey, you need special filtration equipment," Jay notes. "Especially with the wild fruits, the sugar content and pH is all over the board. By making the wines separately and then blending them, we have better control over the taste. The more tightly we control each batch, the more consistent we can be." For some, consistency may be a small mind's hobgoblin, but in the winemaking business, it looms large. "We want people who buy a bottle every couple of months to have it be what they expect. We want them to come back for more."

HARVESTING NATURE

Customers who shop at Minnesota Wild's retail outlet in McGregor can watch the winemaking and bottling process through a large glass window at the wine-tasting bar. Not all fruit products sold by the firm are gathered from the wild. Although there is plenty of wild fruit to gather, it is tough to find people who are willing to pick it for the wages that the market allows. So Minnesota Wild has had to turn first to Minnesota farmers and then, on occasion, to farmers in Wisconsin and Michigan. "If it's not from wild fruit, it won't say "wild" on the label," Jays clarifies. "Minnesota Wild is a brand name, but the wild products say wild plum or wild blueberry on the label."

During the dozen years Minnesota Wild has been in existence, Jay has seen a growing interest in culturing crops like wild plum, chokecherries and high-bush cranberries. The Canadians, he says, have developed the Juneberry — they call it a saskatoon — into a minor crop. As a result, Minnesota Wild has been able to sell small quantities of seeds from processed fruits to nurseries.

"Any landowner can put in a wind break of wild plums or chokecherries," he says. "The worst case scenario is that the birds and bears will have a pile of food, and the best case scenario is that the farmer will get a valuable harvest. The native plants just make so much more sense." Farmers on the Red Lake Reservation have begun raising low bush cranberries. Jay is waiting for the opportunity to purchase part of that harvest.

As his company has expanded, Jay has found that his relationships with Native people, nurtured early in the business' life, have been fruitful in a non-food way. He and Lori have expanded the Minnesota Wild label to include jewelry made at the Red Lake Reservation, willow baskets from Leech Lake Reservation, and birch bark canoe baskets, birdhouses and other crafts from the White Earth Reservation.

All of Minnesota Wild's food and non-food products are available at its retail and mail order store in McGregor and at a variety of specialty shops around the state. The wines, Jay says, are sold to over 100 liquor stores. Jay hopes that as people enjoy Minnesota Wild's products, they will recall fond visits to grandma and grandpa's house, and be reminded of the fantastic ingredients that the wild provides.

RICHARD BRESNAHAN STUDIO
Harvesting Nature Beautifully

Richard Bresnahan is a world-acclaimed potter and environmentalist whose art incorporates materials harvested from nature. Many of these materials are found on or around his 120-acre homestead in Avon, Minnesota. It is here that Richard and his wife, Collete, teach their two daughters and son about the importance of generational continuity and a commitment to environmental sustainability.

Born and raised in Casselton, North Dakota, Richard graduated from Saint John's University in 1976. His final year in college, and the following three years, Richard spent as a pottery apprentice in Japan with Nakazato Takashi, a thirteenth generation potter and son of Nakazato Muan the Twelfth, a National Living Treasure. As a result of his apprenticeship, Richard received the honorary title of Master Potter, the only Westerner to have achieved this distinction from the Nakazato family in its thirteen generations. Richard's work is strongly influenced by the nature-based culture of rural Japan. "One of the most important things about my studying in Japan," he says, "was that there were many elderly people, and people living in the mountains, practicing every day living with nature." Richard credits his Japanese apprenticeship with deepening his appreciation for nature in his art.

Richard returned to Saint John's in 1979 to become an artist-in-residence and to direct the school's pottery program. Saint John's Abbey and University helped Richard set up a totally indigenous pottery studio on campus. Since that time, he has developed the only university program in the United States to fully integrate local and recycled resources with the art experience. Saint John's pottery program educates students and artists in the philosophy and practices of sustainable resource development and involves them in a unique artistic environment within an academic setting.

Richard, his students, and other artists who use the studio create their pottery with clay, glazes, and fuel that come from local sources. While other potters purchase their clay from commercial sources, Richard's clay was dug from a vein he discovered when a county crew excavated a nearby road. A few years later a kaolinite deposit, the material used to make porcelains, was discovered at the Meridian Aggregates Company of St. Cloud. This material was also given to Saint John's. Together, these two deposits are large enough to sustain the pottery studio for 300 years, if the clay is used wisely. Richard explains, "You're only as good as one generation. The whole idea of this is that you don't dig 300 years of clay because you're going to use it up in one generation, you're not living 300 years."

The glazes used on Saint John's pottery also come from indigenous materials. Richard devised a wood-burning boiler system that not only heats his home but provides the means for burning wood and producing ash, which is then collected and stored. The dried ash is mixed with water, refined clay, and feldspar to form a glaze. From his family's farm in North Dakota, Richard collects and burns flax straw, navy bean straw, wheat straw and sunflower hulls. The ash that remains is also used to make glazes. Richard appreciates the range of glazes apparent in his pottery. He notes, "Each plant life pulls out a unique combination of minerals. Each ash glaze comes out a different color."

This balanced existence with nature carries over into all aspects of Richard's life and art. At home, Richard's family practices sustainable forestry. He says, "We have a 100-year forestry plan for the woods here, so we don't cut any live trees down." They only take down the trees that are dead, diseased, or dying, leaving the mature and healthy trees to thrive. Their house, which lies at the center of a hardwood forest, was built completely using beams and boards from trees they milled themselves.

Another testament to Richard's artistic vision is his design of the Johanna Kiln, the largest wood-fired kiln in North America. Named after Sister Johanna Becker, who was responsible for securing Richard's internship in Japan, the kiln is built of recycled bricks and burns only waste wood, not gas. Measuring almost 90 feet in length, the kiln contains three distinct chambers, so that "many artists could benefit from those unique volumes of color palette and flame that you couldn't get from a smaller kiln," states Richard. Temperatures in the kiln reach 2540 degrees Fahrenheit.

Approximately thirty volunteers are needed to chop and haul wood and fill the kiln with almost 12,000 pieces of pottery. The volunteers, led by Richard, work for nearly a month to prepare for and initiate the firing of the enormous kiln. The firing itself takes ten days with volunteers working around the clock. This strong cooperative dynamic appeals to Richard who says, "To have a kiln of this scale, you need a community of people to fire it."

The kiln is fired once a year, a schedule that is at odds with both the academic calendar and commercial systems that require a much quicker turnaround. But Richard believes this is the best ecological and community model for firing high temperature clay. "I'm not so concerned about the object, the end product," he says. "I'm more concerned about the relationships with people, family and, finally, the object's relationship to the planet." Indeed. Richard Bresnahan's life and art continue to be fueled by the world around him and the people in it.

HARVESTING NATURE

WILDWOOD RUSTIC FURNISHINGS
Unique Exports with Heart

Duane Shoup is a highly skilled craftsman inspired by rustic furniture designs and techniques from the past. Crafted from fine hardwoods found in northern Minnesota, his products are unpretentious, one of a kind furnishings with a natural appeal. Duane will custom make a hard-maple rocking chair to fit your unique needs. "I had a guy here last year who wanted a chair, and he came over to my studio to look at one," Duane remembers. "I had one or two sitting here, and he just barely fit in them. So I sized him up, and made one to fit him."

Duane's Wildwood Rustic Furnishings is located north of Itasca State Park in Moose Creek Township of Clearwater County. The mailing address is Shevlin, population 185. "I can have my boat in Lake Itasca in thirty minutes," says Duane. A native of north-western Indiana, Duane left the Chicago area to live in northern Minnesota. "It's a beautiful place to live, but a tough place to make a living. I came up here to live in the woods, but soon realized I needed an export product to make a living."

Voila! All Internet connections lead to Wildwood Rustic Furnishings. Customers access Duane's line of split maple and bent wood custom rockers, rustic pine benches, dining tables and chairs, coffee and sofa tables and accessories through www.wildwood-rustic.com or through the Minnesota Crafted Mall — www.mncrafted.com — a website that showcases Duane's products along with a variety of other Minnesota-made products. People from California order from Duane; people from Outer Mongolia could.

When customers order, they get a product of Duane's artistic vision originally sparked by a 1970s issue of Mother Earth News magazine. Duane saw a picture of a bent wood rocker and directions on how to make one. "I was laid off," he says, "so I thought I'd experiment with it a little." That experiment turned into a successful business.

When Duane walks or rides through the forest, he visualizes finished pieces. He incorporates the natural shapes and bends of the hardwoods into the finished furniture. Often Duane uses downed timber, damaged or already dead trees. He also thins growth to aid larger trees. It is through careful consideration of existing growth that there is a continuous supply of this renewable resource.

Duane's favorite wood comes from skinny little sugar maple saplings. He likes to wander around in the woods with his four-wheeler and specially designed trailer, looking for just the right maple saplings. He is looking for trees that are two to three inches in diameter. Wielding a tiny chain saw, he fells them, bucks them into lengths, piles them on the wagon, takes them home, and peels them with his razor-sharp draw knife. "Maple lends itself well to making this furniture because it's hard and it's strong — it's just indestructible stuff," he says. "And around here it's just considered to be scrap."

When Duane cruises the woods, he looks for nice curves. He likes the liquid harmony of curves. He also likes color. Most of his peeled maple rounds are split in half on his heavy-duty Italian studio band saw. As the saw rips through the hard, dry maple, you can smell the wood. Duane saws the pieces freehand. When he passes a piece through the saw and opens it to the human eye for the first time, most often he sees only the fine-grained, consistent creamy white that has made industrial furniture makers so fond of maple. Occasionally, Duane witnesses a flash of delicate rose or even a swirl of green on a background of cream. Sometimes the heartwood will almost

flow with a rich dark chocolate color. Duane saves the colored pieces for the back and the arms.

"The seat of the chair is the heart of the chair," Duane explains. The legs and the rockers depend on it. The back counts on its strength and it is the sitter's point of focus. " I sculpt out a lot of these seats," he notes. "They're more comfortable that way." The seat is put together with the split and sculpted pieces of hard maple. It is the only place on the chair Duane uses screws. Everywhere else the wood is joined with mortise and tenon or with pegs and glue.

Next, Duane puts on the upright posts and the rungs under the seat. They are all made from round pieces. The parts for the back come from a pile of peeled and split maple rounds the untrained eye would consider crooked stove wood. For Duane, they are parts to a puzzle. He will meticulously sort through a dozen or more, laying them alongside one another, discarding one, adding another, until he is satisfied.

When he is creating the back, he also looks for pieces with a slight concave quality friendly to your back. If it is not there, his band saw will put it there. Flow, harmony, comfort, beauty, all incorporated into a one-of-a-kind piece of furniture crafted to last a lifetime. This Northwoods entrepreneur has created an enterprise that lets him live in and off of the woods that he loves.

WHITE EARTH LAND RECOVERY PROJECT

Putting it Back Together

Aninaatig Zhiiwaagamizigan, gijikonayezigan, manoomin. Maple syrup, hominy corn, and wild rice. These are some of the Anishinaabe words and traditional foods with which the White Earth Land Recovery Project (WELRP) and its retail arm, Native Harvest, are working to make a fractured culture whole again.

Located in an old farmhouse near Round Lake, twelve miles from the village of Ponsford on the White Earth Indian Reservation in northwestern Minnesota, WERLP has a bold vision. Its mission is to facilitate recovery of the original land base of the White Earth Indian Reservation, while preserving and restoring traditional practices of sound land stewardship, language fluency, community development, and strengthening the community's spiritual and cultural heritage.

The vision is bold because the White Earth Band of the Chippewa, or Anishinaabe as they prefer to be called, were granted 837,000 acres (1300 square miles) of magnificent land in northwestern Minnesota by a treaty signed by the United States Senate on March 19, 1867. Over half a century after the Senate signed the binding treaty, ninety-five percent of the reservation had been taken from the Anishinaabe and transferred into non-Indian hands. With the loss of their land, the culture of the Anishinaabe came crashing down upon the people.

"Our land sustains our spirit," explains Winona LaDuke, the founder of WELRP. "The loss of our land has meant the loss of our traditional values." With the land went the language. Along with that went traditional foods and family structures.

Aninaatig Zhiiwaagamizigan, gijikonayezigan, manoomin. Learn to roll those words off your tongue, past your teeth, and out past your lips. Taste the sweetness of the syrup; feel the earth under your feet as you cultivate the corn; hear the mallards as you work through the rice in the fall — and then you might become someone who you thought was lost to you. "What we try to do is put everything together," says Donna Cahill, administrative director for WELRP.

Putting it all together has involved purchasing, or acquiring through donations, 1300 acres of former reservation land. A lot of that land is sugar bush. In

March and April, the sugar bush (woods comprised mostly of sugar maples) bustles with the thirty or so people that WELRP contracts to tap 4000 trees. Later, after thousands of gallons of cold crystalline sap have been gathered, it is cooked down into sweet amber syrup in two large wood-fired sap evaporators. Since it takes about forty gallons of barely sweet sap to make a gallon of syrup, great billows of steam roll off the shallow stainless steel pans, out of the evaporator, and into the woods when the WELRP crew is cooking.

As the crews collect the sap, haul it to the evaporators, feed the roaring fires, and take the boiling syrup off the pans, the children come. And things are put together. "We are always taking groups of children out to the sugar bush, so they can see and learn about their culture. It's important for them to see what their fathers and grandfathers do," Donna says. "When we are out there, we work on language skills too."

Some of the syrup is carefully cooked further and made into tawny brown Anishinaabe Ziinzibaakwadoonsan (maple candy), which the children are allowed to taste. Maybe they can close their eyes and see the brief perfect green of the maple's spring leaves or the flash of hot autumn orange when they taste it. Maybe they can hear the maples sing when they hold that sweet sacrament on their tongue.

"I think of White Earth as my mom's and grandmother's place. It is where they come from. I know that Mom wants to go home and be around trees. My mom listens and talks to trees and if she went home, she'd be happy. I would come home and be happy with her," writes Charlie Boy Thayer in one of Native Harvest's catalogs.

Sometimes the older people associated with WELRP will take the younger people into the woods. That is called jiime. "That's the Ojibwe word for out in the woods," explains Donna."We do that in the spring and the summer. They learn about canoeing and how to survive in the woods. We incorporate language into that, too." In the old days, the families would travel together to make rice camp or maple syrup camp. Nowadays the families are broken and fractured. The children are usually in school. WELRP, working together with the tribal government, is taking the idea of jiime and using it as a vehicle to repair family life. Horses are the vehicles for this work.

"It's fun to watch them with the horses," Donna says. "We have a corral up here and a half dozen horses. It's fun to watch the children come in here, those who have never touched, let alone ridden, a horse, and to see them with the animals. We build our education program around that. We have classroom studies and trail-riding education." The idea is that by learning to work with and communicate with the horses, the children's world will begin to come together. The horses will show how to bring the human families together. "It really works," Donna says confidently.

WERLP sells treasures from White Earth via Native Harvest's catalog and website, www.werlp.org. Some of the money goes to support programs — like hiring an Ojibwe teacher in the Detroit Lakes School and the jiime. More of it goes to paying contract workers, rice harvesters, and wild plum gatherers. Native Harvest's plum jelly is unforgettable.

WELRP also relies on cash donations from individuals and private foundations and the occasional land donation. With those funds, they will buy more land to plant corn for gijikonayezigan, erect a wind turbine on tribal land near the village of Wauban, and put up a new building with solar electric panels for Native Harvest's kitchens and offices. WELRP has allowed people at White Earth an opportunity to stand a little taller and to dream again of a world where everything is put back together.

CHAPTER FIVE
Conservation

Here again, there is 'harvesting' going on, but of a different sort. The human relationship to Earth, at least that of Western dominant culture, has been one of harvesting and exploitation for a hundred years or more in Minnesota. In this section, we come to understand a new harvest of human ingenuity resulting in partnerships without exploitation between mankind and wind power, dairy farming and electricity production, or corporate landscaping and Big Bluestem grass.

This is but one of our challenges in turning the human/earth relationship around. How do we harvest our own creativity, site by site on a human scale, so that we can live in harmony with Nature and so that the Earth's cycles and forces can work with us? How can we let stories of people like the Kas brothers or the Haubenschilds or Ron Bowen teach us how to make a living with the land rather than against it? In addition, how can we leave some of our most precious landscape to future generations? Read on…

HAUBENSCHILD FARM
Putting Waste to Work

Dennis and Marsha Haubenschild run a family dairy farm in Princeton, Minnesota. For twenty years, they toyed with the idea of turning the manure waste from their cows into a useful energy source. Until recently, they rejected the concept because they thought both the risks and costs would be too high.

When their sons, Tom and Bryan, moved back to join the dairy farm in 1997, they decided to increase the capacity of the farm to accommodate 1000 dairy Holsteins. The increase in capacity forced the Haubenschilds to reconsider their waste management system, which eventually led to their long-time dream of turning waste into energy. The dream was no small idea, however, since only twenty-seven manure digesters were operating on livestock farms across the country, and less than half of those were on dairy farms.

The result? Since late 1999, the Haubenschilds have been operating an anaerobic methane digester, which controls odor, creates energy, and provides important soil nutrients for the feed crops grown on their land. Even during the coldest months of the year, the Haubenschild farm produces enough methane from their dairy cows to power their entire farm facility and several nearby homes. "We saved thirty-five tons of coal and 1200 gallons of propane in the month of January alone," Dennis says.

While experts thought the system might pay for itself in ten years, they now expect it to be less than five years. Responding to the success of the digester, Dennis remarks, "I had no doubt that it would work; it just took quite a few years to tie everything together." Initial financing, for example, proved difficult as many traditional lenders rejected their loan requests. With the assistance of The Minnesota Project, a local non-profit, they began seeking assistance from nontraditional sources. Their first success was qualifying for a $150,000 zero-interest loan program that the Minnesota Department of Agriculture developed in 1998. Other state and federal agencies chipped in over $120,000 to supplement the project. The family paid $77,500 in remaining expenses.

High maintenance costs were another potential risk, but the system is proving to require very little maintenance. "We spend a half hour to forty-five minutes per day on maintenance," Dennis says, "And we've had between ninety-seven and ninety-eight percent up-time on the system." At the heart of the system is the methane-fired Caterpillar engine that drives the electrical generator. The components in the engine room include the Cat engine, the electrical generator, heat exchanger equipment, gas and electric monitoring and control panels, and a heat exchanger/exhaust system.

A manure collection and blending pit is under the engine room. 20,000 gallons of manure, along with the recycled newspaper bedding used on the farm, moves underground to the blending pit every day. There it is blended and sent to the digester. The digester is heated to approximately 100 degrees so that the anaerobic bacteria that produce methane can be most productive. The system is designed to cycle a day's manure through the pit in about twenty days.

"The plant is producing more gas than we expected," says engineer Mark Mosser. The reason may be that newspaper bedding is high in cellulose. Cellulose is highly digestible for anaerobic bacteria. Straw bedding, on the other hand, is high in lignin and not very digestible.

"We use 1000 pounds of newspaper a day," say Bryan Haubenschild. "We get it free from a local publisher. All we have to do is pick it up." After the newspaper bedding and manure have been digested and transferred into the manure lagoon, the material is ready to spread. Dennis estimates the largely odorless digestate from the lagoon is worth about $40,000 annually. "The nitrogen is much more readily available than in regular manure," he says. The digestate holds water better and has a pH of 7.4 making it an excellent soil builder on Haubenschild's sandy, slightly acid soils. "Soil is a living thing and the microbial activity of the digestate is very high," he says. "I think it will have a positive impact on soil life," predicts Dennis.

The "biogas" that is produced by the digester is trapped in a dome that covers the tank. The biogas, which contains fifty-five to seventy percent methane, is then directed to an engine and generator that converts it to electricity and hot water. The electricity flows to a transformer as the hot water heats the digester and barn floors. A third of the electricity returns to the farm to power the milking parlor and other operations, while the other two-thirds is sold to East Central Energy, the local electric cooperative.

East Central Energy has agreed to purchase the Haubenschilds' surplus electricity. Minnesota law requires that customer-generators only be paid full retail price up to forty kilowatts. According to Henry Fisher of East Central Energy, the Haubenschilds will produce over 100 kilowatts when fully operational, but the utility will continue to purchase it all at full retail rate. "We view this project as an opportunity to make full use of renewable energy resources and promote sustainable agriculture," Henry says. "We take that energy and roll it into our green power program where we can charge a premium to cover our distribution costs."

The Haubenschilds conduct tours of their facility so that farmers and other interested individuals can see how the digester operates. Encouraging the state to assist other farmers in becoming more self-reliant, Dennis recently testified before the State Legislature to increase funds for manure-processing and odor-control projects. These additional funds would allow farmers with similar dreams to seek interest-free loans to help implement similar projects.

As for their own operation, Dennis and Marsha are delighted with their new system. While it was a long road to travel, they are pleased that all of the pieces fell into place to turn their dream into a reality. Not only has the digester let them expand the size of their farm so that their sons could join the operation, but they are also proud to be on the cutting-edge of renewable energy production.

PRAIRIE RESTORATIONS, INCORPORATED

Minnesota Goes Native

In early March, when winter has yet to loosen its clutch on most of Minnesota, spring has found its way into the Princeton greenhouses of Prairie Restorations, Inc. A busy transplanting crew is putting the first green things of the season — tiny seedlings of plants like bottle gentian, blue cohosh, or pale purple coneflower — into small pots. "Our transplanting crew does thousands of transplants every day," Ron Bowen, the owner and founder of the twenty year old company, says. "The plants go into bigger greenhouses until spring, and then they go to jobs."

A job for Ron's crew might be the establishment of a prairie on a large public project such as a dike being built around Grand Forks, North Dakota, a restoration project on land owned by The Nature Conservancy, the establishment of a prairie and wetland at a corporate headquarters in the suburban Twin Cities, or the creation of a small residential woodland garden. For example, several years ago, Prairie Restorations, Inc. created a forty-five acre prairie at the suburban St. Paul regional headquarters of State Farm Insurance. "Usually when a corporation hires us to do a job, they have a budget and they say to keep within the budget and do a good job," Ron says. "It's a little like hiring an artist. You don't commission an artist and tell them what to paint. You hire them because you like the way they paint."

The artistry of Prairie Restoration, Inc.'s plantings is in ample evidence at State Farm's headquarters in St. Paul. At State Farm, employees and visitors are greeted at the front door by a splash of vivid colors rather than the usual manicured and somber corporate greens of turf grass. "There's no way you'd go into there without saying, 'Wow! this is not just unmowed. This is planted,'" Ron says. "Its full of flowers and very beautiful. There are lots of blue and purple tones, a lot of yellow. It's very diverse."

The corporation saved a quarter of a million dollars by planting forty-five acres of land with native prairie species rather than turf grass. Over the first ten years, the planting, which contains seventy some plant species, will save the company another quarter million in maintenance costs. Ron's crews often perform what little maintenance is needed. Fire is the principal management tool, with a little chemical and mechanical weed control utilized early in the planting's life. "We set up five management zones and burn them alternately over three-year periods, and then we start over again," Ron says. "We use fire to manage quite a few urban sites."

The seeds for creating fields of native plants, or for actually restoring native prairie to something like its former glorious diversity, were planted in Ron when he was a child. At around age six, his family moved to the suburban fringes of St. Paul. "Over the next two or three years, I saw those woods get cut down, the streams put into culverts, and farm fields turned into lots for houses. I felt there was something wrong," Ron remembers.

There were enough of those places left unpaved and uncut to instill in the growing boy a love for things wild and outdoors. As a result, Ron eventually attended the University of Minnesota's forestry school. Instead of cruising timber stands for International Paper after college, he ended up taking care of Senator Mark Dayton's dad's wildflower gardens. Mark's grandmother, Grace,

had been an avid wildflower gardener in the 1930s and 1940s, explains Ron, and her love for the beauty of wildflowers had rubbed off on her son, Bruce. "He knew a lot about wildflowers," Ron says. "Under Bruce, I had quite a bit of free rein. I was able to get a greenhouse, learn how to grow plants and manage seed, and do some early restoration work."

Following a ten-year mentorship under Dayton, during which his confidence and reputation grew, Ron set out on his own. More than twenty years ago, establishing a private business to restore prairie landscapes was a revolutionary idea!

That is history. Now Prairie Restorations, Inc. does prairie, wetland, and hardwood forest plantings and restorations. Besides its Princeton greenhouses and retail store, the company has ten acres of woodlands near Princeton for seed collection from species like trillium and wild geranium, and a 500-acre seed production farm adjacent to The Nature Conservancy's Bluestem Prairie in Clay County in western Minnesota. There is also a contract services base in Cannon Falls so native plantings in the southern Twin Cities metro area can be served. With the recent acquisition of forestland near Duluth, Prairie Restoration will be able to do work in the boreal and coniferous forests of northern Minnesota. During the summer of 2000, the company employed eighty full- and part-time staff.

Growing to this level of success required fortitude. "Seed production farms take many years," Ron says. Bowen collected his first big bluestem grass seed from an abandoned railroad right of way. He explains, "A lot of times you might start with as little as a lunch-bag of seed. You take that lunch bag of seed and you grow it in a greenhouse to get the maximum number of seeds. Then you hand plant those in a row somewhere and they mature — that can take up to three years. When you collect that seed, maybe you have a few garbage bags full, and you plant that. By the end of five to seven years, you might have twenty to thirty acres planted and be ready for commercial production."

Prairie Restorations, Inc. planted its first big bluestem field in western Minnesota, at its Bluestem Farm, in 1991. They harvested 4000 pounds of seed during the fall of 2000. That's enough seed to plant 400 acres. That 4000 pounds of big bluestem, along with Indian grass seed, prairie drop seed, little bluestem, side oats grama seed, and numerous prairie flowers will assure that the Dakota winds will continue to blow across native prairie plants in Minnesota for some time to come.

"I really don't mind turf grass," Ron claims. "There's just too much of it."

MOORHEAD PUBLIC SERVICE
Capturing the Wind

During Earth Week in April of 1998, Moorhead Public Service (MPS) launched its campaign to Capture the Wind®. It took only two and a half weeks for the utility to enlist the support of 425 Capture the Wind® Charter Members. The quick response and tremendous support of these customers led to the erection of the utility's first 750-kilowatt wind turbine generator on the northeast edge of town. The N·E·G Micon turbine, now a local landmark and source of great pride for the residents of Moorhead, can be seen turning throughout the day from most parts of the city. Just recently, Moorhead, residents affectionately named the turbine Zephyr, meaning gentle breeze.

The program works like this. Residential customers subscribe to the Capture the Wind® green-pricing program. In doing so, they agree to buy either all or 1000 kilowatt-hours per month of their electricity from wind generation and agree to pay a half penny more per kilowatt-hour to finance the cost. Customers agree to participate for an initial three-year period, followed by one-year renewal periods. For a typical Moorhead resident with 1000 kilowatt hours of energy consumption per month, the program adds five dollars to their utility bill. For that five dollars, the participant prevents 8800 pounds of carbon dioxide, the most prevalent greenhouse gas, from being emitted into the atmosphere. "That is equivalent to planting 1.2 acres of trees, or removing a car from the road each year," explains Chris Reed, director of energy services for MPS.

Commercial customers may also participate in the voluntary program by purchasing either all or a block of 1500 kilowatt-hours of electricity at Capture the Wind® rate. An average commercial customer will pay an additional $7.50 per month to participate in the program. By agreeing to purchase 83,000 kilowatt-hours of electricity each month at the Capture the Wind® rate over a period of ten years, nearby Moorhead State University is the utility's largest customer participating in the program. Moorhead currently receives two-thirds of its electricity from hydropower and one-third from a coal-fired power plant. The wind power will displace coal generation for participating customers. "Wind power is renewable and affordable," says Bill Schwandt, MPS general manager. "Wind turns the turbine rotators, that spin the generator, that makes electricity. No need to mine, burn, or dispose of anything."

Not only did it take less than a month to fully subscribe MPS's first green-pricing program, but the enormous support left the utility with a waiting list of about 100 customers for the next installment. In late 2000, Moorhead launched its "Help Moorhead Capture Its Second Wind" campaign and in less than one month, the utility gained enough support to build its second wind turbine generator. "Everywhere I go, people stop me and ask when the next turbine will be built," notes Chris.

Excitement for wind energy has grown tremendously after the first installment. The turbine is a highly visible success; it is nearly always on-line and has had almost no mechanical problems. Moorhead has also received wide recognition for the success of their project, energizing the community and participants. Ken Norman, the president of the MPS Commission, says, "To get such quick and enthusiastic support from the customers of Moorhead Public Service the second time around, shows that the people of Moorhead are eager to increase their efforts to bring more renewable energy to our community."

Chris attributes the initial success of the program to the strong relationship between MPS and its customers, a low cost premium, an educated and

enthusiastic community, and unwavering support from the environmental community. Simply put, says Chris, "If you want the program to work, price it fairly and ethically, and be straight with the customers." A little more quietly, he will admit that the utility also had a clever marketing program. First, they picked a catchy name and logo — both of which are now widely known around the country in energy circles. Second, MPS direct-mailed every customer inviting them to be a Capture the Wind® charter member and held a high-profile press conference to further encourage Moorhead residents to become involved.

Most importantly, MPS worked carefully to make sure each person received proper recognition for his or her part in advancing renewable energy in Moorhead. In return for signing on, each member has had her or his name displayed on a plaque now mounted on Zephyr. Members also have access to Capture the Wind® T-shirts and baseball caps, pins and pinwheels, and pictures of themselves next to the turbine. The Capture the Wind® newsletter is sent to members semi-annually and focuses on the advancement of the program. Chris explains, "The people who committed to paying more for their electricity deserve credit for the Capture the Wind® program and should be recognized. We want to give them something tangible in return for their money."

The enormous support of the Capture the Wind® members has gained much national attention for the utility's green-pricing program. With more than seven percent of its customers supporting the program, MPS now has the highest customer participation rate in the country, according to the National Renewable Energy Laboratory (NREL). The Capture the Wind® program is also recognized by NREL for having the third-lowest premium for a wind energy program. And because of the successes of its Capture The Wind® program, MPS was awarded the 2001 Energy Innovator Award from the American Public Power Association in June of 2001.

The utility's second turbine is scheduled to come on-line in October 2001. Like the first wind turbine, the massive structure will roll into town on at least six separate semitrucks. The tower alone will take three semi-beds and will loom over the town at 180 feet. Like Zephyr, the large blades on this turbine will rotate at a relatively low speed of twenty-eight revolutions per minute, reducing the risk of injuries to birds often associated with earlier turbine designs.

Like the first, this second turbine is likely to generate interest among community members and tourists alike. Two years after the installment of the first turbine, Chris finds himself conducting tours at least every other week for Cub Scouts, local school groups, renewable energy advocates, legislators, and other interested parties. He has also been helping local schools use the Capture the Wind® experience to bring a renewable energy focus to their education.

As to why he helped pioneer one of the most successful community wind projects in the country, Chris remarks, "We're a municipal utility; we're owned and governed by our customers. A significant portion of our customers has an interest in where their electricity is coming from. If our customers want a program and are willing to help support it, it is our job to offer the program."

RAINY RIVER MONITORING PROGRAM

Collaborating for a Fishable River

"You can not separate a water body in half. The Rainy River borders the two countries, but one country cannot act without having it affect the other side — it is all connected," explains Jennifer Mercier, environmental services coordinator for the Rainy River Band of Ojibwe. The band is spearheading a unique water-monitoring project on the Rainy River — a waterway that borders Minnesota and Ontario, Canada. In cooperation with Jennifer, teachers and government workers, students from both sides of the border work together to monitor the water quality in the Rainy River. The program has formed lasting partnerships across borders and has set in practice what community members on either side of the river have long talked about.

The program took root some years ago when the Elders became concerned that Band members were calling themselves "protectors of the Rainy River" but were not acting accordingly. At the same time, members of the community on both sides of the river had become alarmed over the deteriorating health of the Rainy River. Large paper mills on both sides of the river, water levels, fishing pressure, and land use along its banks all contribute to the concern about the river's water quality. In an attempt to change course, the Elders asked Chief and Council to do something — to stop talking and start acting. After identifying their mission, "to protect, conserve and revitalize the Rainy River through education, monitoring and rehabilitation," the band hired Jennifer Mercier to breathe life into their goals.

On the U.S. side of the river, Koochiching County had been developing river management plans for three of its major rivers, including the Rainy River. Along the way, county workers developed a model program where children test and monitor water quality as part of their schoolwork. Richard Lehtinen, director of environmental services for the County, recognized the opportunity to join the two efforts and began applying for grants. "The problem with non-point source water quality monitoring is that no one has the time or resources to do it consistently. By setting up a monitoring program in the schools, it becomes an ongoing program. We were able to find a couple of $5000 grants that covered the costs of the necessary equipment, and now the program is virtually self-sustaining because it is part of the school curriculum," Richard explains.

Jennifer now leads teams of fifth and seventh graders from both countries on field trips to learn about the river, collect data and monitor the river quality. In both the fall and spring, seventh grade classes go out to the river with Jennifer. They get their hands dirty and learn how to do water sampling and environmental tests themselves. One of the favorite water tests involves bugs. "Bugs can indicate river health. If the kids find a sample with only leeches and bloodworms, for example, they know the water quality may be only fair to poor. Leaches and bloodworms are relatively pollution tolerant. If they find a sample with bloodworms, leeches, dragonflies and mayflies, however, they can infer that the water quality is better because dragonflies and mayflies are pollution intolerant," explains Jennifer. "The children love the bugs — they think they're cool. They even enjoy hearing stories about the bugs, like how mayflies are only found in a certain season and generally only live for one day," she continues.

Another part of the monitoring program is an experiment. "The students put fathead minnows in flow-through containers — also called two-liter pop bottles with holes poked in them — and leave the minnow filled containers in the river for a few days as a type of low-tech, sub-lethal toxicity test. Depending on how many minnows have died by the time the children return to investigate their containers, they may draw rough conclusions about the toxicity of the water. Of course there are lots of variables in an indirect test of this type, but if there are persistent deaths in an area we may be able to point to a specific problem," she notes.

While Jennifer works on developing monitoring projects for the younger students, Lynn Hoffmann, the industrial arts teacher for the Indus School, has pioneered a full-year course for high school students. The older students can run more complicated tests that the other students cannot yet do and because it is part of the curriculum, the high school students work on developing techniques and systems for the years to come. "We have seven different sites where we do various tests which include: pH, temperature, dissolved oxygen, conductivity, turbidity, nitrates and total phosphorus. Some of the tests are a little erratic, but we're learning. We began talking about sampling the tributaries and the kids got excited about that. Now they want to add new sites and we're almost getting in over our head!" Lynn explains with a laugh. "The kids took a real interest in it. They kept coming up with new things they wanted to test and new ideas. I think it is really unique that our district helps us do this," he adds.

Students not only learn about science and the environment as they collect the data, they are contributing to an important and growing data bank of information about the river. The children's data are compiled and explained to them and then shared with government and other agencies. "We have two main objectives," states Jennifer. "One is trying to get kids interested in science and to raise their awareness of the river. It gets them concerned about conservation and gives them a chance for hands-on learning." The second objective is to collect data. "If we do this for ten years, we'll have good baseline data about the river," she explains.

Jennifer's neighbor to the south, Richard Lehtinen, explains that two small grants from the Minnesota Department of Natural Resources and the University of Minnesota Northeast Minnesota Sustainable Development Partnership gave the project life. Interested teachers on both sides of the border make it a success. "This is a grassroots citizen effort," Richard explains. "Because we have teachers who are interested in incorporating this into their curriculum, we can have an ongoing program for the price of the equipment." And adults involved hope the program has a rippling effect, inspiring some students to pursue careers that they might not have otherwise. "When students apply the information they learn in textbooks to a real life problem, the information takes on a whole new life," states Richard. "This is a way to assure better water quality over the long term. The Rainy River is a real resource," he adds.

The vision of the members of the Rainy River Band of Ojibwe, coupled with the leadership of Jennifer, Richard and Lynn and the unbridled enthusiasm of the children has made the borderless partnership a success. "We have been able to build the capacity of a watershed community to deal with these issues. Building partnerships is where our greatest strength lies," explains Jennifer.

KAS BROTHERS
Planting a Twenty-five Year Crop

From one perspective, Richard and Roger Kas of Woodstock, Minnesota, are typical Midwestern farmers who grew up farming the family land with their father, William Kas. However, this family has something unmistakably unique taking place on their farm. They have seventeen modern wind turbines on their land, generating enough electricity to power 3000 average households, and they're about to put up two more. What is even more unique is that the Kas brothers will own these two new commercial-scale wind turbines. This is the first project of its kind in Minnesota, and possibly in the whole Midwest.

Wind development came about in southwest Minnesota after the State Legislature mandated that Northern States Power (now called Xcel Energy) contract 425 megawatts of wind generated electricity by 2002. Landowners quickly signed leases giving the utility and wind development companies rights to put wind turbines on a portion of their land. The Kas family was part of this group of landowners.

Roger and Richard chose their developer carefully. The first seventeen turbines on the Kas family's land were developed by Dan Juhl of Danmar Associates. Roger explains, "I wanted to get a project on our land. Dan was here first and we talked, but we had an agreement that if someone else came up with a project first and made us a good offer, we would go with them. There were no exclusive agreements."

While Juhl was working to put his project together, he kept in close contact with the Kas family. He kept them up-to-date on the different aspects of planning, permitting, negotiating a power purchase agreement, and arranging the financing. The process took a long time. It was 1993 when Dan installed

an anemometer tower to measure the wind on the Kas farm. And it was 1999 when the seventeen machines were completely installed and producing power. The machines take six acres out of crop production on the Kas family 320-acre farm. The life of the machines is expected to be about twenty-five years, as is the purchase agreement.

Roger paid attention to how the project came together on his land. He may not have an equity position in the Juhl project, but he certainly has an interest in its success since his wind easement annual payments are based on a percentage of the gross revenue from each machine. Roger says, "Farming the wind is not right for everyone. We're here every day feeding the cattle and taking care of the farm, and we see the wind turbines as just a few more machines for us to take care of. In that respect, you need to learn about the machines and take care of them just as you need to know how to take care of your crops and livestock." Roger, who has worked on and off in construction all his life, was hired for six months by Vestas, the turbine manufacturer, to work on construction and machine maintenance when the Juhl project was being installed on his farm. This work gave him valuable experience. Roger explains, "If you want to farm the wind, you should have the knowledge of how it all works."

Over time, the business relationship between the Kas brothers and Dan Juhl grew. They now have completed the planning and financing for a second project which the Kas family will own. "Right from the start, I thought, if the big companies can get in it and make a go of it, the little guys can too," says Roger. Juhl led the way on the Kas brothers' project, in part, because he had done it before and knew the path. He also wanted to help forge the way for a different type of project, one that is farmer owned and farmer built.

"This is possible on a small, individual scale, but this is a commercial venture, it's not a hobby," says Dan. Because the project is under two megawatts, the Kas brothers are not required to perform an environmental impact study. Also, Dan negotiated the Power Purchase Agreement with Xcel for the two megawatt project. "This is an essential part of the project; this contract is the guaranteed long-term revenue for the sale of wind generated electricity, and this is what the capital financing is based on," explains Dan.

The brothers worked with Dan to arrange the financing. It took more time than a normal farm loan. They had to give extra information to the local bankers to bring them along and get them interested in the wind project. It was all new to the lenders. Richard and Roger have put twenty percent down on the loan and eighty percent is financed with the Power Purchase Agreement as the loan guarantee. The multiple years of wind data and Juhl's project performance were evidence of the strength of the wind resource. "Some land is better for raising corn and soybeans, some is better for wheat, and other places for rice," says Roger. "In the same way, some land is better for wind. The wind resource has to justify the capital investment."

Roger knows he is forging the way with his project and knows that some

things will be much easier for the next person to put up a wind project. He insists "I am not giving anyone any advice now. I can't give any advice until our project is up and running." But both Roger and Richard hope that some day soon they will be able to share what they have learned with other landowners interested in harvesting the wind.

Lutsen Scientific & Natural Area

A "Whole Great Gift from God"

Ask Lloyd Scherer if he spends much time in the woods, and you'll get a laugh. "It's my life," he says. Posing the question to Lloyd is not unlike asking Magic Johnson if he's ever spent time on a basketball court. A person would be hard pressed to find someone who knows the north woods better. For most of his adult life, Lloyd has spent winter days, backpack slung over his shoulder, traveling through the Lake Superior Highlands in Cook County. Now 82 years of age, it is still a rare day that does not find him exploring the mysteries of the northern old growth forest. "Even the same place," he says, "is different every day."

While raising his four children as a single father, Lloyd founded a nursery and landscape business that left room for exploring between the fall freeze and the spring breakup. He would roam for days at a time, following the pathways deer and moose lay down and often traveling by snowshoe — so often that he has worn through three pair. Today Lloyd has turned his hand to art, and he paints wilderness scenes on birch bark, framed and sold at a Grand Marais gallery. Ever curious, Lloyd continues to walk the woods almost daily, and always observing the new mysteries of the northern wild country.

In 1991, Lloyd made an important contribution to the future of the highland forests by donating a 240-acre parcel of land to the Scientific and Natural Areas (SNA) Program of the Minnesota Department of Natural Resources (DNR). It was land that he had carefully acquired in three separate parcels, the first in 1968, and the others following in the 1970s. His family lived sparingly so that he could purchase this land he knew was valuable: valuable for its relatively undisturbed old-growth communities of northern hardwood, northern hardwood-conifer, and upland white cedar forests; for the home that it offered to wildlife; and for its beautiful Sawtooth Mountain setting. He bought the land to protect it from development, hoping one day to pass it along intact to his children.

For more than twenty years, Lloyd's land remained virtually undisturbed while elsewhere in the region residential and commercial development was changing the landscape dramatically. These changes had an indirect but no less dramatic effect on the Scherer land. As land values in the area began to rise, property tax assessments rose right along with them. Lloyd had no intention of selling the land for development, but his taxes increased regardless.

When Lloyd came to believe that the inheritance of the land would represent a financial burden to his children, he began to look into other options. After consulting with a number of conservation organizations, he invited SNA Program supervisor Bob Djupstrom to join him on a walk to view the property. Bob was impressed by the land's old growth forest and value as habitat for rare plants. The land was clearly a good candidate for designation as a state Scientific and Natural Area.

For his part, Lloyd appreciated the high level of protection that SNA status would offer the land. Unlike other preserves, there is a strong provision against any new development on SNA lands and many of them do not even host hiking trails. He liked the idea that such undisturbed areas served to provide baseline scientific information that would be used to increase understanding about managing other natural areas in the state. He had found the right recipient for the donation of the land he treasured

and he made certain his children agreed. "For them, it was worth more than any inheritance from me," explains Lloyd.

The SNA program has done well by Lloyd's gift. The donated 240 acres were used to create the Lutsen Scientific and Natural Area, which less than two years later was tripled in size by the acquisition of adjacent land. The additional acreage had been acquired through a land exchange by the non-profit Trust for Public Land (TPL), which sold the land to the DNR at half its value, donating the remainder. Through the Reinvest in Minnesota Critical Habitat Match Fund Program, both the Scherer donation, and the TPL donation, qualified for matching funds, which go to acquire or improve existing land that is critical wildlife habitat. Donors thus double the conservation value of their donation. The Lutsen SNA is now a full 720 acres — one of the largest preserved old-growth forests in the state.

Today Lloyd is site steward for the Lutsen SNA and quietly guards the land against overuse. If people begin trafficking the area, it will no longer be what it is today," he cautions. Because of Lloyd's thoughtful stewardship, Minnesotans can enjoy knowing there is at least one place where pine marten can find calm shelter in the bases of fallen old-growth trees and where timberwolves can bed down without the fear of human interruption. With its assortment of large diameter sugar maples, yellow birch, and white cedars (some of which are believed to be 300 years old). the Lutsen SNA protects a priceless piece of the North Shore's natural heritage.

Lloyd Scherer is a man of modest means who could have realized significant income had he sold this land. But for Lloyd, the land was not about money. He puts it this way: "We don't actually own land; we are entrusted with it. Inevitably, we must pass it on to the next generation. We should be ever thankful for it and the water and air that sustain our physical lives, and use them only with care and respect, never arrogance. All life shares this earth with us. We should love this whole great gift from God."

CHAPTER SIX
Tourism & Culture

Hospitality is an age-old concept, and here it includes sharing with travelers the unique sense of history and place that each location exudes. When thinking in these terms, tourism is all about location, as these stories — north and south — attest.

From Mille Lacs, where we learn just how close modern life still is to its indigenous roots, to Plainview's new theater, the reader may wonder with the Mississippi Headwaters Hostel manager whether to share or keep the secrets of this vast and diverse state. But when the generosity of the human spirit is combined with the uniqueness of place, magic happens. Travel becomes far more than "getting away" and evolves to "getting into" communities, histories, and ecosystems.

Travel through these stories, keeping your ear tuned to the way art and tourism combine with the help of the human spirit. When a proprietor or community designer thinks at this level, the result is true hospitality.

Moonstone Farmstay Bed & Bagel

Cared for and Welcoming

Not long ago, most Americans had relatives or friends who lived on farms. Those farms were often summer vacation destinations — the rural lifestyle, the escape from the city, the space, the animals, the plants, the bugs! As fewer and fewer people farm, and as Americans get further removed from their agrarian roots, the family vacation to a farm has slowly slipped away.

Audrey Arner and Richard Handeen would like to change that. Having traveled in Europe and experienced agritourism firsthand, Audrey and Richard set out to pioneer the concept on their farm in Montevideo, Minnesota. A farmhouse in the countryside, serving as a bed and breakfast for urbanites, is big business in Europe. With a 240-acre farm on the gently rolling blufflands of the upper Minnesota River Valley, and a landscape that is home to humans and cattle, corn and alfalfa, beaver and coyote, coneflowers, big bluestem, evergreens and hardwoods, Audrey and Richard saw no reason why agritourism could not work in Minnesota. In 1999, they opened Moonstone Farmstay Bed & Bagel.

Their brochure reads, "The Broodio at Moonstone Farm is a one-room cottage that is part of our Minnesota River Valley century farmstead. The simple pleasures of the prairie include awakening to songbirds and the occasional lowing of cattle." The Broodio, a former "brooder" house (for raising young chickens) that had been converted into an artist's studio, has now been transformed into a cottage for guests. It is pleasantly decorated in warm tones and features original artwork, solar technology, traditional and handmade furniture and fresh flowers in season.

Audrey and Richard serve their guests organic coffee, or farm-raised herbal teas, and a continental breakfast is available. Visitors can walk through flower gardens and orchards, skip rocks on the pond, or cross-country ski on trails at Moonstone Farm or at nearby Lac qui Parle State Park. Bathing facilities are nearby in the main farmhouse, or guests may use the outdoor privy — just down the garden path.

Audrey and Richard see the Bed & Bagel as part of their vision to host a flow of people through their lives and livelihood. "We tend to have a lot of guest traffic generally, and decided to extend ourselves and capitalize on hospitality," says Audrey. Audrey and Richard now enjoy a widening circle of people who appreciate country life, seek respite from the noise of the city, want to learn about sustainable agriculture, or want to recapture something of a long lost farm of their youth. The Broodio is a good addition to their enterprise.

In 2000, their first full season, Audrey and Richard had a gentle, steady flow of guests during the growing season — one or two guests a week staying for one to three days. Most visitors came from the Twin Cities, in town for meetings or vacationing. Audrey and Richard have had guests from New York and a few international visitors. People learn about them by word-of-mouth, through the Montevideo Chamber of Commerce, and through Prairie Waters, a regional agritourism initiative that produces a publication called *Fun in the Country*.

People come to Moonstone for different reasons. Some guests like to be reclusive and work on unfinished poetry and music. They come for the privacy and quiet. Some guests want to help with farming projects. "We've had people help with mulching, fencing, painting, and moving cows," Audrey says. "People seem to like a real-life alternative to generic motel rooms," she adds. "They like to learn about other farms in the area that direct market market their products to customers, area artists, or historic sites."

either get bigger or get out all together. For Audrey and Richard, it made sense. Half of their acres were several miles away and traveling back and forth with equipment stretched them so thin that the additional income did not make up for the time lost.

Traditionally grain farmers, Audrey and Richard added livestock to their operation. They saw this as an important decision, both in caring for the land and adding profit. They now raise pasture-fed beef and direct market the meat to consumers through the www.prairiefare.com website. Audrey and Richard still raise grain, but much of it they now raise organically. Their experiments over the years with cover crops and reduced tillage have provided a basis for a flexible approach to crop production.

That Audrey and Richard are pioneers in agritourism is not surprising; after all, they have been forging new paths and making changes to their farm for the past ten years. Through her work at the Land Stewardship Project, Audrey was introduced to Holistic Management® as a tool to manage a farm and landscape. Her enthusiasm for the concept inspired others in her family, and they decided to try the process on their farm. The process entailed the extended family sitting down together and hashing out what was important to them in terms of managing the farm. Initially, the process was uncomfortable for some family members. "Part of me felt, why do we need to talk about this; haven't we been doing fine up to now?" Richard recalls. But in the end, everyone was pleased with the result — a set of clear goals that guide their farm management and enable the family to have the quality of life they want.

The result of the process is a diversified operation that includes crop farming, raising livestock, running the Bed and Bagel, and being thoughtful stewards of their land. Audrey and Richard have scaled their farm down from 480 to 240 acres, a rare occurrence in a farm economy where people

Audrey and Richard are also committed to enhancing the natural environment at Moonstone. They have planted evergreens, hardwoods, and fruit and nut trees. They have built retention ponds and planted native species to support and attract a variety of fish, amphibians, birds, mammals and insects. "We think of our place as a water 'catchment' area," Audrey and Richard agree. "Most of the rainfall that is not absorbed by our landscape runs through grassland before entering Moon Creek." This direct tributary of the Minnesota River is one of the thousands of small streams that constitute more than ninety percent of the Minnesota Basin's waterway-miles.

By diversifying their farming enterprise, Audrey and Richard have been able to stay profitable and achieve their desired quality of life. By opening the Moonstone Farmstay Bed and Bagel, they share their passion for farming and the land with others. Their attitude is summed up by the greeting on their website, "Welcome to the farm we have the privilege of caring for."

MILLE LACS INDIAN MUSEUM
A Confluence of Old and New

Ken Weyaus, Sr., can teach us how very close we still are to the traditional Ojibwe that lived, hunted, and fished in Minnesota just decades ago. As he leads tours through the Mille Lacs Indian Museum and Historic Site on the western shore of Lake Mille Lacs, he will say, "There's my aunt in that photo. And that's my family in that photo." This is both his personal and tribal heritage. Ken himself used to live part of the year in a wigwam selling Indian crafts during the summer, yet he is intentional as he teaches that one should not be left with the impression that traditional lifestyles are still practiced in the old land-based, seasonal ways. A rolling conversation with Ken Weyaus is in itself a blend of the old and the new.

In much the same way, a confluence of diverse energies created the Mille Lacs Indian Museum on Highway 169 between Onamia and Garrison, Minnesota. The museum itself is nearly fifty years old as a formal museum, and the artifacts inside it have been collected in this very spot, on the shore of the big lake, since almost the turn of the twentieth century. Yet it was a combination of leadership and funds from the Mille Lacs Band, the Minnesota Department of Transportation, the Minnesota Historical Society, and from individuals and local foundations that allowed the beautiful domed structure to come into being in May of 1996.

In 1914, a trader by the name of D.H. Robbins opened a trading post on this location and traded with all peoples, Native Americans and early white settlers in the area. In 1918, Harry and Jeanette Ayer bought the trading post from Robbins. These traders and gardeners had been raised in the Twin Cities and trained in the School of Agriculture at the University of Minnesota. Their shoreline businesses grew to include a trading post and store, tourist cabins, and a boat-building factory.

In October and November each year, the Ayers would close their business and travel to the Southwest, trading with Indians and bringing back art and artifacts. By 1966, when the Ayers passed away (within a few days of each other) 4000 Native objects had been collected and were, at that time, donated to the Minnesota Historical Society. Among the artifacts were museum-quality, hand-painted dioramas about traditional Indian life.

By 1981, local leaders made the decision to build a larger museum to display and teach with the artifacts. Full planning did not begin in earnest until 1991, when six leaders from the Mille Lacs Band and six from government agencies, plus architects and Historical Society leaders, began actively designing the new museum. Meetings continued nearly monthly for over five years, and money was steadily raised from public and private sources.

A beadwork design was replicated on the outside of the building. The center of the building, with a higher ceiling, was at first designed to look like a drum. However, as Ken recalls, "the structure started resembling an oil refinery, so the center roof was then domed, as it is now, wigwam-like with elm bark." Building costs increased from an estimated four million dollars in 1981 to an actual ten million in 1996, yet by then the community was growing and was up to the task. Artifacts were recovered, restored, and the traditional dioramas were repainted and once more pulled together. The museum opened with a huge community potluck on May 18, 1996.

Inside this beautiful wood structure, one sees the confluence of old and new. Native beadwork from generations past is prominently displayed. Interactive computer stations teach about the role of the Mille Lacs Band of Ojibwe in the modern life of their community, such as the use of casino funds to strengthen the Onamia community for its members and its non-Indian neighbors. Veterans are highly respected in Ojibwe culture, and a section of the museum pays tribute to veterans through visual displays and audio-education. The displays of Pow-Wow regalia connect one to both the beauty of traditional dress and the continuing art of dance practiced today by the Ojibwe.

Most dramatically, the center high-dome structure of the museum houses the traditional dioramas — life-size stations depicting Indian life season by season. Beginning and ending with winter in this circular space, each station shows the housing and life of the people, living close to the land and off the land's bounty. A winter teepee leads to spring sugar bush, leads to summer wigwams near the shores of the lakes. By autumn, wild ricing activity dominates. And in winter, families moved again deeper into the protection of the forests and lived off of their harvests as well as hunting and fishing. These life-like scenes include models of Native people, and not surprisingly, Ken knows them! "There, that is Rose Benjamin," he says, or "that woman is my aunt, Cecilia Dorr." Ken's stories bring all of the traditions into modern day focus and remind us how very recent that history really is.

A restored 1930s trading post stands next to the museum and offers a variety of books, crafts, and clothing. Currently, the Mille Lacs Indian Museum brings in travelers and local folk and teaches them Ojibwe crafts. The museum features local artists like Margaret Hill, a generous craftswoman skilled in many arts using birchbark and sweetgrass. This lovely, sunny and welcoming building is full of art, history, music, hospitality, and good humor.

Showing his playful nature, Ken clicks into one of the interactive computer stations teaching the Ojibwe language. Clicking on the word "food" and then an icon of a pie, a woman's voice speaks the Ojibwe word for "blueberry pie." True to the cumulative nature of this language, this word likely teaches the entire recipe for blueberry pie, and who knows, maybe even the location of good berry-picking! Here is the word for "blueberry pie" — Minibaashkiminasiganibiitoosigianibadagiingwesijiganibiitooyiingwesijiganibakwezhigan! Ken teases that this is why he never ate blueberry pie as a child — he did not want to have to say the word to ask for it!

HARVEST FESTIVAL
Fresh Food and Family Fun

Every autumn, on the shores of Lake Superior, something special happens. Regional farmers, local artisans, and urban neighbors come together to enjoy food, family, crafts and music. It all began in 1990, when a group of farmers, social justice activists, and local church members created the foundation for the first Local Changes for Global Solutions Conference. The goal of the conference was to provide a forum to discuss environmental, peace, and justice issues. One of the outcomes was the Harvest Festival, held annually since 1994.

The Harvest Festival brings producers and consumers together in Duluth for a day of fun. A family-oriented outdoor event, the Festival attracts thousands of visitors each year. Visitors feast on locally-produced food and enjoy the farmers' market, crafts, demonstrations, youth activities, exhibits, and live music — complete with a solar-powered sound system! A giant vegetable contest is a visitor favorite, as are the petting zoo and the demonstrations of traditional crafts such as soapmaking, blacksmithing, fiber spinning, and maple-sugaring.

In the exhibit area, festival-goers can learn about the efforts and resources of local and regional organizations. The cost? Free! Visitors only need to bring an appreciation of the fine fare offered by local farmers.

"We hope that this annual event can help to develop a healthy and sustainable local food system in the area," says Jenifer Buckley, the event's organizer. The festival brings together regional farmers who are dedicated to production methods that use fewer pesticides and synthetic fertilizers, that reduce soil erosion, protect water quality, treat animals humanely, and that increase the diversity of the area's food production.

In addition to linking farmers with customers, the event is also educational. The event organizers want consumers to leave with a better understanding of the benefits of a local food system. "When people buy locally grown produce and meat, jobs stay in the area," says Jenifer. "Energy use is reduced because food is not shipped thousands of miles, and rural areas benefit from keeping dollars and people in their communities."

By highlighting local and regional farmers and their produce, the Harvest Festival hopes to restore farm culture, too. The goal is not to develop an idealized image of life on a farm, but to promote real life examples of sustainable methods of farming. "We want to educate current farmers and potential farmers about alternatives to mainstream farming practices," Jennifer says.

The Festival showcases some of the highest quality produce in Minnesota. From cucumbers to parsnips to sweet corn to tomatoes to peppers to herbs, and much more, the amount of produce available is astonishing. Joel Rosen, a local farmer and an active member of the Sustainable Farming Association of Northeast Minnesota, speaks of his experience at the festival: "It's amazing the shock on people's faces when they bite into something fresh and naturally ripe," he says. "The sugar content just blows them away."

Festival participants are all committed to caring for the land and using envi-ronmentally sustainable methods. They are also committed to regional alliances and the formation of markets for their products. Joel believes that there is a social element to sustainable agriculture. "We are attempting to create a lifestyle that works for families and one that future generations might be able to choose for themselves," he says.

While the Harvest Festival has grown, the message has remained the same — by bringing urban and rural people together for a day of fun and new experiences, all those involved learn about sustainable agriculture and its benefits. "A community harvest festival can have a powerful effect on a community," says Joel. "It can reinvigorate the link between farmers and consumers." Whether it is enjoying a bowl of Joel Rosen's famous gazpacho, eating an ear of sweet corn or a slice of pumpkin cheesecake, or watching demonstrations and listening to music, the Harvest Festival is a great event for people of all ages.

RURAL AMERICAN ARTS PARTNERSHIP

"That's Our New Theater"

Sometimes art begets art. On his drive home from a poetry festival in Marshall, Minnesota, in the spring of 1998, Ken Flies imagined the basic idea for the Rural American Arts Partnership. He had heard enough that week of abandoned barns and falling silos, and he knew there was a strong rural culture alive in and around Plainview, Minnesota. He and his wife, Millie, had recently decided to relocate to their homeland of Plainview, so Millie could open a restaurant and Ken could spend time writing.

Maybe it was Ken's love of writing and his high school acquaintance with author, Jon Hassler. Perhaps it was his background as a marketing and planning executive with several start-up companies or his work with the Peace Corps and community development. Or maybe it was simply his powerful imagination — but Ken knew it could be done. Ken sat down and wrote a mission statement and business plan for a rural arts partnership. Ken and Millie then pulled together a small group of people including Dean and Sally Harrington, and Sally Childs, artistic director for the (then Minneapolis-based) Lyric Theater. It did not take

them long to start envisioning, in detail, the multi-program rural arts partnership Ken had conceived.

The Harringtons, who long dreamed of a theater in Plainview, added energy and enthusiasm to the project, and Dean applied his financial expertise as a banker. Dean was aware that a project like this would not attract Minnesota arts funding until it had some sort of track record, so early theater productions were scraped together. Meanwhile, local donors became interested enough to help with the down-payment on a building. The Partnership began pilot productions and carefully tracked where interest and audiences came from. "We saw that Rochester was a good market, and in summers the Twin Cities — especially for Hassler productions," says Dean. The local community was not far behind the metro areas as an important audience base.

Sally Child's connection to Plainview and the Rural American Arts Partnership lies in the Lyric Theater's ten-year history of producing Jon Hassler's work and her experience in developing stage pieces out of the work of regional

"People and events just started falling into place," explains Ken. The enthusiasm still shines in the eyes of its founders, as they share details of the birth of a theater. In addition to hard work, the effort has also had its share of good fortune. For example, the theater procured all of its 225 seats at no cost. Ken Flies tracked down the seats at Augustana College in Sioux Falls from a campus theater, just before it was torn down.

Adaptations of novels have proven to be the most popular so far, and the Hassler Theater Company will produce works by rural Minnesota writers as well as classic works like *The Fantasticks* and *On Golden Pond*. *Simon's Night*, by Jon Hassler, ran in 2001 and *Grand Opening* will again appear just before Christmas. All on Broadway – and in plain view!

The theater also adds excitement and practical experience to the local high school's creative arts programming. Students work on lighting, build sets, and audition for parts. Local adults also get involved; a dairy farmer from the Rochester area does the lighting work for winter performances.

poets such as Bill Home and Leo Dangel. Minnesota novelist, Jon Hassler, grew up in Plainview, and at least one of his popular rural stories was set there. "Hassler's book, *Grand Opening*, is about life centered around a local Plainview grocery store in the late 1940s," explains Sally. It made sense to transfer the work of the Lyric Theater from Minneapolis to Plainview and to work together with the Partnership. It also seemed right that the new arts center was to be named the Jon Hassler Theater, and that the first play featured was based on *Grand Opening*.

The Hassler Theater, "on Broadway" in Plainview, is built in a simple structure formerly housing an International Harvester dealership. It had the "right footprint" and "owners who were enthusiastic about having the building become a theater," says Sally. She also brought in Erica Zaffarano, a set designer, to assess the building for staging plays. The theater is now a spacious, easily accessible 225-seat production facility.

As the theater became a reality, other segments of the Rural American Arts Partnership fell into place. The Methodist Church came up for sale, and the Arts Partnership saw it as a potential space for a history center. Before long, it also became known that Hassler's boyhood home (the house itself) was soon to be demolished. Not so. The Rural Arts Partnership bought it and moved it one lot away from the theater. "This will be the site of a new writer's center — a place for writer's conferences, book clubs, a small retreat facility, and a program for in-resident writers," says Ken. "We want it to appeal to all ages — school-age youth to older folks."

Many of the elements of the Rural American Arts Partnership are in harmony with the community's broader vision for itself. A bike trail, a recommitment to its history and culture, a new organic restaurant called Rebekkah's, the Tavern on the Green with its capacity to handle large dinner groups (Ken and Millie's successful venture) — all make sense together. The Partnership board and town leaders feel that the whole rural experience is what will appeal to tourists, and that parts of southeastern Minnesota are still well-kept secrets. The Partnership's mission is just as thoughtful as its leaders are: to preserve and promote agricultural-based rural and small town American culture and values, through history and the arts.

Here is a setting within two hours of the Twin Cities that offers rolling countryside, lovely church steeples, proximity to the Kellogg Weaver Sand Dunes area and the beautiful Whitewater and Carley State Parks, small shops, and now the arts.

Have there been any surprises? Possibly the buy-in of the local townsfolk. Stories abound describing early skepticism that has evolved to full-blown pride. "That's our theater," they say, and season tickets are not a thing reserved for trips north to the Metro area or south to Rochester. A few core people believed in this, and energy now runs high. Theater embedded in rolling farm country is, for Plainview, just the beginning.

MISSISSIPPI HEADWATERS HOSTEL

A Best Kept Secret

Nestled in the heart of Lake Itasca State Park just 400 feet from the park's busy bike and boat rental concession, the Mississippi Headwaters Hostel is one of about 140 hostels in the United States. The hostel, which is on the National Register of Historic Places, was built in 1924 as Lake Itasca State Park's first headquarters.

Tom Cooper, who has managed the hostel for the last decade, thinks it is one of the best kept — and most economical — travel secrets in Minnesota. Some days, Tom would like to keep it that way. On those days, he takes a long ski or hike through the pristine forest around Lake Itasca before returning home to a crackling fire in one of the hostel's eighty-year-old stone fireplaces. Tom's job is to promote the thirty-one bunk hostel and maintain its financial viability. "Our biggest problem is that hostels are not well understood in this part of the country," says Tom, who discovered hostels while traveling in Europe. "We get calls from people who ask us if we have running water and indoor toilets!"

"I just don't get it," Tom says. "People will go to Douglas Lodge (the state-owned park lodge) and it will be full. The people at Douglas Lodge will tell them about us, and they won't even check us out. Maybe they don't like cooking for themselves." Maybe not, but many guests do enjoy cooking in the hostel's kitchen and having their meals in the dining area, with its old maple floors, log beams, stone fireplace, and spectacular view of Lake Itasca. Guests can also stay at the hostel and take their meals at Douglas Lodge.

According to Tom, large groups often rent the entire hostel or the eighteen-bunk south wing. There, for a very reasonable price, guests will find a congenial living room with skylights and three small dorm rooms furnished with the hostel's solidly made Vermont maple bunk beds. Beyond the sitting room and bunks of the south wing is a game room. But unless it is raining, most visitors want to be out canoeing, hiking, swimming, biking, skiing, snowshoeing, or just soaking up the magnificence of Minnesota's oldest state park. The entire floor plan of the hostel can be seen at its website: www.himinnesota.org.

Although most guests of the Mississippi Headwaters Hostel tend to be family groups in the summer and ski groups in the winter, the hostel nicely accommodates couples or individuals. Most of the rooms have six bunks, but there are smaller rooms of four and five bunks. "The last time my wife

are from faraway places. "I once met a Russian mother and her daughter who were traveling around the world together," recalls a visitor. "There were also a couple of young Finnish girls. Then just last weekend, Tom had visitors from Australia."

Hostels belong to the people who use them, and that sentiment is reflected in hostel customs. "At hostels, we operate under the belief that you are responsible for yourself," Tom says. That means if you make a mess in the kitchen, you clean it up. You wash your own dishes and wipe down the tables. And when you leave, it would be nice if you vacuumed your room. The idea is to leave the hostel as clean as you found it.

Most hostels inhabit historic buildings located in spectacular settings. In Minnesota, there is another one on an island near the Boundary Waters Wilderness Area. Just over the border in South Dakota, there is one in a renovated barn in a wooded valley. In California, there are a couple in lighthouses perched on cliffs hovering over the Pacific's surf. The Mississippi Headwaters Hostel, which is managed by the non-profit Minnesota Council of Hostelling International, has both the spectacular and the historic. "When was the last time you talked about the history of a chain motel out on the highway?" Tom, sipping his coffee in the dining room, asks a visitor. But then not many chain hotels are on the National Register of Historic Places or located at the headwaters of the Mississippi.

and I stayed at the hostel, we had one of the smaller rooms, the Antonia DeMichiel room, all to ourselves," a recent visitor says. "Actually, on a crystal blue January week day, we had the entire hostel to ourselves. Truthfully, we had Itasca Park's thousands of acres largely to ourselves."

Part of the fun of hostels is meeting interesting people. Because the hostel is part of an international network, some of the interesting people who visit

CHAPTER SEVEN
Community

Perhaps the Texan and Mexican farmworkers featured in this chapter say it best: "People united will never be defeated." This section brings us stories of such unity of mind or spirit.

"Community" is built when people come together, recognizing their individual talents and diverse abilities or viewpoints as assets, and when they co-habit time and place. Here we learn of community built to alter oppressive living conditions or to create a quality regional food supply. Action is motivated by hope, beauty, or human need. Community forms around a region of the state, environmentally-sound business values, or the handwork and patience of special people brought together on the land.

When humans unite in these ways into a sense of community, what results is a powerful force. In these many locations, for these many reasons in our fine state — may it be so.

CENTRO CAMPESINO
"Unidos" in Owatonna

Centro Campesino headquarters in an upstairs office building in downtown Owatonna, Minnesota, not far from the town's central square. This non-profit, membership organization was formed by migrant farmworkers in response to problems they faced in their working and living conditions. A conversation with Centro Campesino organizers is sprinkled with poetic phrases, phrases of hope — *Hasta la Victoria* — until the victory. Through organizing, advocacy, and service, Centro Campesino works to improve the lives of agricultural workers and rural Latinas and Latinos in southern Minnesota.

How many American consumers, when they purchase a simple can of green beans, are aware of the story behind that product? For more than sixty years, *campesinos* (farmworkers) have traveled the 1476 miles from southern Texas and the Mexican border region to live, April through October, in southern Minnesota's migrant camps. Tens of thousands of workers pick vegetables or fruits, work in food-processing factories, earn low salaries, and live, during these months, in migrant camps where sub-standard housing is typical. *Campesinos* encompass a demographic group that suffers a disease rate six times higher than the norm and an average life span of forty-nine years.

Imagine producing 6300 cans of vegetables per pallet times 100 or 120 pallets per twelve-hour shift. Imagine returning to your camp at six a.m. only to switch places with your spouse who will work the next twelve-hour shift. Imagine trying to rest while caring for your children, then returning once

again to your own twelve-hour shift, belts running at higher speeds if a profit margin or incoming crop is pushing the system. Imagine this seven days a week for fifteen or more weeks during the peak-processing season. On-the-job accident rates are as high as twenty-five percent. As Jaime Duran remembers, "A two-person job was reduced to one. The machine kept going, and I was doing the impossible. I never dreamed the machine would pick me up and put me through it — but it did."

Controlled by *contratistas*, or crew leaders, the workers had not, until the late 1990s, organized locally in response to this situation. As one leader put it, "a spirit had not awakened in the people to dispute these conditions." In 1997, Campesino leaders, with support from the Center for Urban and Regional

Affairs at the University of Minnesota, conducted a detailed survey of all farmworkers in the region. A majority of the families participated and revealed facts and opinions that later set the tone and mission for Centro Campesino.

After a thirty to forty hour drive from southern Texas, only four percent of those surveyed describe the migrant camps in which they arrived as "comfortable." Seventy-eight percent mentioned problems with restrooms in the camps; twenty-seven percent were concerned with the quality of the water. Fifty-three percent explained that transportation to and from the jobs was the biggest problem they faced, and with sixty-five percent Spanish speakers, more than half surveyed wanted interpreters available to facilitate communication with their bosses.

At the end of the 1999 harvest season, committee members developed a strategic plan for the organization under the training and guidance of Baldemar Velasquez. A small group of farmworkers then stayed in Minnesota during the winter of 1999-2000 to build the organization and raise money. Community meetings were held, and farmworker families began to see that this effort, self-organized by their own people, offered hope. By the summer of 2001, eighty percent of *campesino*s had joined Centro as members.

Leaders of Centro Campesino work steadily and incrementally for such things as storm shelters, hot water in the camps, or remodeled day care facilities. They also speak of the whole system saying, "people want to be respected. There is a feeling of waking up, of wanting to know their rights. We focus on the truth of the truth."

Organizing is done carefully. If an employer is pressed too hard, they may simply move the production elsewhere. These are global companies looking for the cheapest labor, and campesinos promised work. A food-production system that demands this profit orientation is a justice issue of the biggest scale. "This is not just one issue," says one of the leaders, "we all have a responsibility to make the entire system more just. I hope that Minnesotans understand the faith that we have, and that they support us in making change."

One energizing story surrounds the Willow Creek Intermediate School in Owatonna, benefiting for the first year from Latino/Latina liaisons. Teachers at the school have been trained to see the full cycle of the lives of farmworker families, to see the full scope of the situation. Liaisons help improve the reading ability of migrant children, assisting staff over a language barrier. In the spring of 2001, the entire school focused on Mexican culture and history, ending the school year with a fiesta that included all students.

Organizers take pride in their logo, designed by a fourteen-year-old migrant worker. Rooted in Mexico with "*fe*" or faith, the stalk of the corn plant travels up the map on the route of Highway 35, through "*esperanza*" or hope in Texas and to "*justicia*" or justice in Minnesota. Four corn leaves represent the four states traveled through on the journey north. Minnesota's arrowhead region forms the beak of an eagle, and a raised fist standing for solidarity or "Union" forms the tassel of the corn and the crown of the state. Campesinos who travel north with hope in their hearts, and who bring their muscle and determination to the food system in Minnesota, are working to find justice — decent working and living conditions — at the far end of the journey.

By joining together, the campesinos in Minnesota believe they can bring about change. *El pueblo unido jamas séra vencido* — the people united will never be defeated!

CAMPHILL VILLAGE
Many Hands Make Light Work

Established in 1980, Camphill Village in Sauk Center, Minnesota, is an agriculturally-oriented rural community that includes adults with developmental disabilities. Part of a large network of villages around the world, Camphill is dedicated to fostering an atmosphere of confidence and mutual appreciation amongst community members. The first village in the network was founded by Dr. Karl Koening in Aberdeen, Scotland. Koening's vision was to focus on the abilities of people, not their disabilities. Today, Koening's vision flourishes at Camphill Village Minnesota and in over ninety communities in nineteen different countries.

At Camphill Village Minnesota, there are seven houses, a woodworking shop, a weavery, a flock of chickens, a beef herd, large crop fields, gardens, woods and prairies. Echoing Koening's intent, the community is deeply rooted in natural and agricultural cycles. Most of the crops are grown organically, and the community responds to the cycles of the seasons. "We plan out our work schedules every six months based on the changing of the seasons," says Mary Davis. "In the summer, there's the garden, processing kitchen, and farm crops, so we are outdoors more."

There are about seventy community members at Minnesota's Camphill Village, and each resident is an integral part of the community. Take, for example, the bakery crew. Brenda Steves, who has washed dishes in the bakery for many years, comes in to work at nine o'clock. Working her way around the large kneading tables (crafted in the Village workshop years ago) to a sunny part of the bakery, Brenda prepares for the morning's chores. Brenda cannot hear nor speak, but she greets Sarah, a fellow villager with Down's Syndrome, with an affectionate rub on the back. Jan Zuzalek, having already prepared the dough the night before, has returned to finish her work. Danny, who can only speak a few words, has been working at the Camphill Bakery since its inception over twenty years ago. Danny, like Brenda, exudes enough good-naturedness to brighten any room.

Once the crew is assembled, the bakery becomes a place of focused industry. Each member of the team is keenly aware of both his or her own responsibilities and the responsibilities of others. Jan and Sarah oil the bakery's well-seasoned bread pans. Brenda proudly washes the large dough pan from the night before.

Sarah kneads her bread with gentle firmness, flattens it with her palms and then rolls it into a loaf and carries it to the pans. She is efficient and fast. Brenda, now finished with the morning dishes, also helps knead. "She kneads a loaf with one hand and then gives it to me to finish," says Jan.

Within fifteen minutes, a dozen loaves of weighed and kneaded whole-wheat bread are nestled in the loaf pans. By ten o'clock, a dozen Dakota wheat loaves are tucked away in the warmer oven to rise. The finished product is proudly fed to the members of the Camphill community, and sold to customers in Sauk Centre and the Twin Cities.

Jan believes there is a healing aspect associated with the community's bakery. Part of that healing comes from performing the meaningful work of providing the Camphill villagers with a wholesome staple food. "Just getting your hands in the warm, moist dough has its own therapeutic effect," she says. According to Jan, "We raise our own wheat, and it's really important to make our own bread with it. Camphill is an agricultural community and baking bread is an agricultural act."

Other community members are responsible for tending to the fields, working in the wood shop, maintaining the grounds and buildings, and caring for the livestock. For community festivals, the musical talent from within the community is pooled together into a band that, according to Sarah, plays really good music!

At Camphill, Sarah is called a "villager" whereas Tom Farr is called a "co-worker". Sarah is said to be a person with "special needs". But Tom knows two things; that Sarah has unique needs that require special attention from other people to be met and so does he. Tom knows that

"special needs" exist on a continuum and on some days it's not clear where he exists on that continuum.

In the words of the Camphill Association of North America, "Members of the communities teach and learn from each other in a process of mutual interaction. The needs of each person are met through living in a cooperative community — each individual contributing his or her own special gifts and talents."

Camphill Village Minnesota is a place where people with special needs, like Sarah, Brenda, and Tom too, can experience life, enjoy a community of good friends and family, learn skilled trades, and express their talents. It is a good place to be.

ANGRY TROUT CAFÉ
Where It All Comes Together

Plates of succulent Lake Superior trout and herring draw people to the Angry Trout Café in droves. Beyond the extraordinary food, customers also leave knowing that they have participated in something revolutionary.

Since its inception in 1987, owners George Wilkes and Barb LaVigne have made thoughtful changes to the way they do business in the little town of Grand Marais, Minnesota. Inspired by Paul Hawken's book, *Ecology of Commerce*, George and Barb have modeled their business on the cycles of nature. They have found ways to reduce waste and have developed local sources for the food and products they use in the restaurant. "It dawned on us that this was a creative opportunity to link our environmental ideals with our business," says Barb. Along the way, the two found other benefits. "Making good environmental choices has become an avenue to better business," says George. "It has a positive effect on our marketing, quality, and costs."

While waiting for a table, guests can peruse piles of reading material on sustainable agriculture, fair trade, and sustainable businesses. George and Barb have detailed their plans and business philosophy in the Angry Trout Environmental Business Statement. In their words, "By involving ourselves in our business's effect on our community and environment, we are better informed as to what is truly valuable and good, and that helps us to identify what is most profitable now and especially into the future. A more sustainable Angry Trout Café is a more efficient, marketable and successful Angry Trout Café."

This sentiment has not been lost on the increasing numbers of customers loyal to the Café. When the restaurant switched to organic chicken and vegetables, Barb found that some people came specifically because they could get organic food. "They know our business is trying to address some important issues, and people appreciate that," Barb adds.

Simple, high-quality food is the key to the success of the Café. Eighty percent of the vegetables served are organic. Barb's strategy for buying organic is to buy in season and to shop around. "The organic vegetables that are reasonably priced are the ones that are in season," she explains. Sticking with in-season vegetables helps the Café maintain high-quality food and adds variety to the menu. In spring, yellow beets grace the salad and tender asparagus complements the meal. Later in the summer, zesty red peppers spice up the salad and Minnesota-grown sweet corn arrives with the meal.

To keep the quality of the food high, George and Barb do not serve meat from factory farms. "It is no accident that environmentally-responsibly grown chicken tastes better and is better for you," George explains. The chicken served at Angry Trout are organic, free-range chickens raised by Organic Valley Farm Cooperative, located in southwest Wisconsin. George and Barb's neighbors, Harley and Shele Toftey, who dock their commercial fishing boat next to the Angry Trout, supply the Café with herring. Fishing operations in Grand Portage, Minnesota, provide lake trout and whitefish. Salmon is caught off Alaskan shores, flash frozen, and shipped to the restaurant in returnable containers.

George and Barb are also continually trying to improve on a series of waste reduction ideas that are designed to save money and conserve resources. A local gardener composts the Café's vegetable waste, and table scraps are delivered to nearby friends to feed their sled dogs. They even switched from bottled beer to kegs to further reduce waste. "We were waist-deep in empty beer bottles that had to be recycled. It was a nightmare," says George.

George and Barb have struggled with the waste of take-out packaging for some time. "For three years, we refused to have take-out, but that was bad for customer relations," says George. In order to respond to the demand, they decided to try a returnable, reusable take-out container and supply it at no charge. Customers leave their name and phone number, and return the container later. The process is working well so far, and customers have thanked them for the effort.

George and Barb have made a few changes to reduce energy and water use, but would like to do more. They have installed compact fluorescent lighting, low-flow water faucets, and a super-efficient Sun Frost freezer, which uses half the electricity of a conventional freezer. The Café also uses half-sized, organic cotton napkins that reduce the water and energy needed for washing. "Some people laugh when they see our tiny napkins," Barb notes.

"One of our biggest challenges is energy use — because of all the cooking," says George. He is collecting information about high-efficiency stoves and ovens, and researching the possibility of incorporating wood-fired or bio-fuel cooking equipment in the kitchen. George and Barb also purchase approximately twenty-five percent of the cafe's electricity from a wind-powered generator located in southern Minnesota.

The Angry Trout's owners believe that an important step to sustainability is to connect with the local economy when possible. The Café has become a showcase for the northwoods, and northwoods artists. Lake Superior pebbles lie embedded in the floor. Tables are crafted by local carpenters out of fifteen different native tree species. The chairs, complete with fish ladderbacks, are made of local birch.

Local builders, using wood sawn at the local mill, constructed the timber frame addition. The roof design includes shingles made of northern white cedar. A fish chandelier, made by a local metal artist, greets guests in the waiting area. The same artist recently finished fish sconce lighting and outdoor deck furniture. Dinnerware is handmade by Dick Cooter, a potter in Two Harbors, Minnesota. Paintings by local artists grace the walls. Maple syrup, hand-harvested wild rice, berries, bread, fresh herbs and vegetables come to the restaurant from the surrounding area.

George and Barb are using their community's unique resources to build a business that grows towards sustainability, is profitable, and offers a customer-friendly atmosphere. Local resources, from sled dogs to master carpenters, are what make the Angry Trout Café more than an excellent restaurant. In the words of their Environmental Statement, "Sustainability is rapidly becoming the competitive edge of the future."

NORTHEAST MINNESOTA SUSTAINABLE DEVELOPMENT PARTNERSHIP

Local Citizens and the University of Minnesota Working Together

Tucked among serene pines at the Cloquet Forestry Center, is a beehive of activity called the Northeast Minnesota Sustainable Development Partnership (NMSDP). The Partnership is reaching out to a wide range of groups in the region to find innovative ways to renew the countryside. With the energetic support of its executive director, Okey Ukaga, the Partnership combines citizen leadership with the research and education resources of the University of Minnesota to foster long-term sustainability in the northeast region of Minnesota. The Partnership focuses its efforts on opportunities connected to agriculture, natural resources and tourism. This Partnership is one of five in Minnesota that are each supporting vital work in their regions.

Policy and the Great Plains Institute for Sustainable Development, a project was initiated to collect stories of sustainable development from across Minnesota and publish them in this book, *Renewing the Countryside*, and on a website (www.mncountryside.org). Near MacGregor, at the East Lake Center of Mille Lacs Band of Ojibwe, a community garden project is underway. Participants share in the rewards of successfully producing organic fruits and vegetables.

While the University of Minnesota is best known for educating students and granting degrees, it is also a research institution, and much of the research that takes place at the University benefits the citizens of the state. Direct input from citizens into the University's research agenda, however, is not common. In certain fields, like agriculture and natural resources, citizens increasingly feel that corporations and federal granting agencies have too much influence on what research is pursued. David Abazs, NMSDP board member, explains. "The Partnership helps bring the community into the driver's seat by empowering members of the University to do sustainable work as opposed to research often tailored around corporate interests."

With funding provided by the people of Minnesota via the state legislature, the Partnership has helped start or has given critical support to a wide range of projects. For instance, landowners on the Gunflint Trail received assistance in dealing with thousands of acres of forest blown down in 1999 windstorms. Community members, Landscape Architecture faculty, and the Regional Rail Authority worked together to develop designs and plans for the Virginia and Eveleth segments of the Mesabi Trail, a major recreational trail crossing northeastern Minnesota. In partnership with the Institute for Agriculture and Trade

Okey uses the term "active citizenship," which means local citizen participation in identifying, designing, and implementing projects in their region. Not only are citizens energized, but faculty members who see the need for citizen input are enthusiastic. "It has unearthed a lot of sincere University individuals who have been quietly working for similar goals and objectives despite the pressure of meeting the conventional University expectations," says David.

The history of the Regional Partnerships can be traced back to active citizenship both inside and outside of the University of Minnesota, working

together to develop a model of partnership. The NMSDP was one of three pilot Regional Partnerships and the process involved citizens from the start. Board members were identified through a nominating process, and members were selected to provide geographic and issue area representation. The board then interviewed and selected the executive director for the Partnership. And that was just the beginning — all projects that the Partnership supports must address issues identified by and of concern to local people.

Developing networks of cooperation is also a primary role of the NMSDP. An example, is the Northland Food and Farming Initiative. At the Partnership's first annual planning retreat, community food systems emerged as a key interest. In response, a team was formed to develop a plan, and the Northland Food and Farming Initiative was formed. This initiative is working to increase the use of locally produced food in Northeast Minnesota and Northwest Wisconsin and strengthen the infrastructure necessary to do this. Many people are involved in the process, including University of Minnesota — Duluth professor Dave Smith.

Dave, who teaches Human Ecology, has his students, as part of their coursework, do community projects related to food systems. Students have interviewed people developing farmers' markets, talked to restaurant owners and grocery store managers about using locally produced food, and interviewed farmers about their work and the future of local farming. One student recalls, "I experienced a shift in my reality — that my research project was not just academic learning, but a real effort that was being made by real people to put into practice the sustainable values I have learned in the classroom and through books." The information that students gather is developed into reports that help direct the work of the Northland Food and Farming Initiative.

Building true partnerships is not easy, as the NMSDP board members have learned. "It's been like searching in the dark for a common understanding of sustainability and then moving projects into action," explains David Abazs. What makes the Partnership effective is that it lives up to its name. The partnerships that make this project a success include the one between the citizens and University of Minnesota faculty members on the board, and those between the organization and the surrounding community. "We are trying to foster a rich and vibrant relationship between citizens and their Land Grant University," says Okey.

COMMUNITY

ROOT RIVER MARKET

Cooperation Rooted in Houston

"It's kind of hard to see a small town die," says dairy farmer Doris Henderson. With that modest understatement, Doris and dozens of other diehard residents of Houston, Minnesota, have created a community-owned grocery store and pharmacy. The 7000 square foot store, called the Root River Market, is dedicated to community development and the nearly 1000 residents of this southeastern town. "Business is pretty good," Doris says. "People really like the quality of the meat, and I hear lots of good things about the pharmacy. Houston hasn't had a pharmacy for twenty-five years."

In the 1950s, Houston had five grocery stores. When the last, an IGA store, closed in fall 1998, the town residents did not throw up their hands in despair and say, "That's progress." At first, they did what Americans do everywhere — they waited for the government to step in. "There were efforts on the City's part to try to get someone to come in," Doris remembers. "But it's a small enough market so that the larger groceries didn't want to mess around with it."

Houston residents responded with a fine trait found in so many communities across America — stubborn determination. Driven by that sentiment, they did another very American thing, they held a meeting. Community "newcomer," Peter Denzer, having lived in Houston for only ten years, called that first meeting a round-table discussion. He hoped, perhaps, to fool the old-timers into showing up. And he succeeded.

"We need to thank Peter as the person who got the concept going," says Doris, whose family has lived in the area over 140 years. "He's very much interested in seeing small farmers keep going and in promoting a strong small town economy." Out of the round-table discussion came a commitment to have a grocery store in Houston, more meetings, and a board of directors for

what would eventually become the Root River Market. "Among us all, there was a common interest in doing something to serve the community," Doris says. "There was also a strong interest in eventually creating a market for locally-produced, high-quality food."

One of the first steps was to incorporate, and then put together a business plan. Board member and tax accountant Larry Connery was instrumental in putting the plan together, however, no one knew much about organizing or operating a grocery store. Technical and financial assistance came from Hiawatha's Pantry, a non-profit organization working on local food systems in the region. "The Board is a remarkable mix of people with diverse qualities," says Nancy Bratrud, coordinator for Hiawatha's Pantry. "I'm hopeful that the whole community will rally around the store. We see in Houston what could be a workable possibility in other small communities."

Getting other Houston community members involved is exactly what the new board of directors set out to do. To kick off the cooperative's membership drive, the board held a chili supper in a vacant grocery store in July 1999. The board, along with the local Chamber of Commerce, rolled up their sleeves and fed a few-hundred community members. The result? Over two-hundred families became members, paying $100 each for membership.

"At first we had a hard time convincing people that a food cooperative was not a health food store," Doris recalls. "We told them they'd be able to buy Campbell's soup and Jiffy peanut butter. Some people wanted to wait to see what happened. We told them, if they waited, there'd be nothing to see." Eventually, the cooperative signed up over 400 members, but that was not quite enough. To get the store up and running, the board needed $400,000. "For a dairy farmer, that's a lot of money," Doris says.

Root River Market raised another $150,000 from the community by soliciting loans from individuals and businesses. Two of the businesses that loaned the new cooperative money were other cooperatives in the town. "They understood that one of the principles of cooperatives is to work together," Doris says. The balance of the funds was raised in the form of loans from North Country Cooperative Development Fund, the National Cooperative Bank, and a private regional bank.

With solid financial backing, competent management, and a strong board of directors, the cooperative is moving

beyond its initial phase. "The original concept of the market includes education as well as selling," Doris says. "People want to know where their food is coming from, and we want to serve that need." As a step in that direction, the Experiment in Rural Cooperation, one of the University of Minnesota's Regional Sustainable Development Partnerships, worked with the board and others to put together a plan for a regional food system that will supply local grocery stores, including Root River Market, with locally-produced organic foods of the highest quality.

Root River Market is committed to maintaining its close connection to the community. When Sharon Onsgard, one of the founding board members and a retired teacher, died before the store opened, the sign for the Root River Market — three pine trees standing together — was dedicated in her memory. Like the pine trees, standing together with the community is what will make the Market a lasting and valuable asset to the residents of Houston.

CHAPTER EIGHT
Learning

It is fitting that this final section in Renewing the Countryside focuses on our society's youth. In five stories, young people learn through direct hands-on experience and often directly with nature. Here we read not only of experiential learning, but also of excellent models of teaching and mentoring. These are small scale and local ideas put into action with youth and art, youth in business, youth gardening or young people learning natural resource management. Here also are two stories that remind Minnesota of its indigenous beginnings — seeds to sugar bush. These stories may inspire us to remember that alongside all daily activities must run a thread of attention to the upcoming generation.

The human spirit's connection to young people is similar to our personal connections to land or water or cultural heritage. May we renew ourselves by staying alert to all stages of life — to past and future generations. May we remember and gain hope, knowing that these creative young people will one day lead us.

HARVEST MOON COMMUNITY FARM
Arts, Earth & Farming

Harvest Moon Community Farm gets positive marks from the children who participate in its programs. "We made a lot of things from nature." "I learned to draw like a real artist." "We got to go pick corn; it was my first time going into a cornfield!" Teachers reinforce Harvest Moon's work, too. One teacher remarks, "For the past two years, I have had the opportunity to bring thirty students to Harvest Moon. Each time we visited the farm, it was an extraordinary experience. The students, who are usually surrounded by the sights and sounds of a city, are exposed to rural living. This new environment stimulates questions and discoveries not possible in their regular setting."

Located near beautiful Scandia, Minnesota, Harvest Moon Community Farm was founded in 1996 by Ann Rinkenberger, its current executive director. As a non-profit organization, Harvest Moon provides children and families opportunities to explore the arts and their connection to nature in a rural environment. "Building an awareness and appreciation of natural and agricultural resources are integral pieces of each program," says Ann.

Harvest Moon began as a Community Supported Agriculture (CSA) farm that served local and Twin Cities' families. In its first year, it offered a variety of vegetables, herbs, and flowers. It also educated its members about how to use produce and about issues surrounding sustainable agriculture and living simply. Based on the success and interest generated by its educational programs, a decision was made to focus on educating youth, teenagers, and adults about living more sustainably.

Harvest Moon offers a variety of popular programs. The Create and Cultivate Art Camp provides six through eleven year-old children with an opportunity

to work with artists. Students make art using products that are sustainably-grown on a farm, gathered from nature, or represent agriculture or nature in the final product. The June 2001 program included puppetry with In the Heart of the Beast Puppet and Mask Theatre, making beaded story bracelets, creating sculptures, and weaving. The August session included photography with Doug Beasley, book making, felting wool and Taiko drumming. At the end of camp, the students' works are showcased at an art show that features the projects each child made and music or theater performances. "The children love it," says Ann. "They get a chance to be outdoors, be creative, and take pride in their work."

Another program at Harvest Moon is the Create and Cultivate Farm Camp. Here, children ages six to eleven learn about sustainable agriculture, farm animals, environmental preservation, organic gardening, and the arts. A day at the camp might include listening to a sheep's heartbeat and comparing it to a chicken's; learning about how sheep are sheared; and learning how wool is washed, carded and spun into yarn. On another day children will make a simple solar cooker from a box, black paper, tin foil and plastic wrap, and then enjoy a great snack after watching how the sun cooks pizza and s'mores!

Then there is ArtVenture, an after-school arts program held off-site at Scandia Elementary and Forest View Elementary schools in Washington County. At ArtVenture children from kindergarten through sixth grade learn about arts, sustainable agriculture, nature, science, cooking, gardening, and physical education. One day's activities might include creating an agate picture frame with gemologist Scott Duncan, learning about the formation, mining and polishing of collected minerals, and getting materials and directions for making stalactite or stalagmite rock candy at home with their families. Each lesson has a different focus, such as arts, gardening, or the environment.

In addition to educational programs, Harvest Moon publishes a newsletter, offers programs for families, and maintains a website — www.hmcf.org. All of

Harvest Moon's activities highlight farming, rural communities, and home-steading lifestyles in the St. Croix River Valley. "By integrating people into life on a farm, Harvest Moon hope to help young people and adults develop stewardship values, skills, and the ability to care for natural and human communities for many years to come," says Ann.

BOLT ENTERPRISES

Entrepreneurship — Sixty Gallons at a Time

BOLT Enterprises thrives on doing things "unconventionally". To begin with, their CEO is only eighteen years old — and this isn't an Internet company. BOLT (Business Opportunities through Learning and Technology) Enterprises is a student run business that produces, markets, and sells Prairie Smoke Bar-B-Que Sauce. It is one of the first programs in the state to give students the "school-to-work" experience by having them create and run their own business. It all happens at Westbrook-Walnut Grove High School in Westbrook, Minnesota.

It started when school board member, Jim Schmidt, discovered Rachel Green's Smokin' Barbeque Sauce on a trip to Colorado. Green had been making and selling the sauce to restaurants, but did not have time to keep up with the demand. Through contact and discussions with Schmidt, Green agreed to allow Westbrook-Walnut Grove High School to make the sauce.

The school's Business Applications class, taught by Lynn Arndt, took on the challenge. The result is BOLT Enterprises and the ongoing production of the fabulously successful Prairie Smoke Bar-B-Que Sauce. In its first week, BOLT sold 250 of the 389 bottles of barbeque sauce it produced. By the end of its first summer, the students had sold 2200 bottles of sauce and had already bottled 6000 more. Prairie Smoke was sold at local events, such as the Laura Ingalls Wilder Pageant, through the summer of its first year.

BOLT currently sells product to local businesses and homes, takes mail orders and continues to grow. They have expanded their product line to include two new flavors of barbeque sauce, hot and honey. While the Cabela's sporting goods store in Owatonna, Minnesota has sold the Bar-B-Que Sauce for a couple of years, BOLT now ships the sauce to all Cabela's stores across the country. In addition, BOLT has designed a special gift box for Cabela's stores. Students hand craft two-pack wooden gift boxes with the Cabela's logo on the side.

Students are responsible for every aspect of the business, from setting the business up for operation and creating a board of directors, to bottling, promoting, and marketing their product. In the process, they have learned about lobbying, licensing, research, trademarks, nutrition, and marketing. Karie Evirst, former student CEO of BOLT, says, "We feel like we've been exposed to virtually every aspect of the business world. We have negotiated with big companies, purchased materials on a commercial scale, and have learned the skills and techniques it takes to communicate with others in the business world."

the vat and their supplies. All of the sauce is made in the school kitchen by the school's cooks, then bottled, capped, and heat-sealed in an assembly-line process by the students. Once the bottles cool, a label — designed by two students — is applied. Each bottle of sauce is then offered for just under four dollars.

The students conducted their own market research and offered taste tests at school events. "It's been a lot of work, but everyone has been very supportive," says Corrinne. "The community, teachers, parents, and students have all been behind us. It's really exciting." It is also an empowering experience for students. "When we come in wearing suits and ties instead of jeans and t-

The opportunity not only trains future entrepreneurs, it provides important employment for rural youth. Profits go to help finance scholarships for seniors at the high school. "It's students helping students," says past student board chair, Corinne Parsons.

shirts, people do take us seriously," says Dennis Kleven, reflecting on working with adult professionals. "They treat us with respect."

When the project began, students sought advice from state legislators and local business groups. Westbrook-Walnut Grove High School received a $5000 grant from the Southwest Minnesota Foundation, $1400 from local donations, and got help from the Agricultural Utilization Research Institute (AURI) to launch BOLT Enterprises. AURI helped the young entrepreneurs get licensed, obtain nutrition information, and standardize their recipe.

BOLT's board of directors includes students and school officials. The 1999-2000 board was made up of five students, including the student president, vice-president, and secretary along with two student representative "members at large." The adults included members of the school board, the high school principal, the Business Applications teacher and an accounting teacher. Though board members change, the excitement for the business and its success is seen in each new face.

BOLT Enterprises produces all of its sauce in a sixty-gallon vat bought, along with the ingredients for the first 1,000 bottles, with the donations and grant money they received. Each batch makes enough sauce for 370-380 bottles. They have also built a small addition to their high school's kitchen to house

BOLT Enterprises began in 1996 and has held strong, succeeding a little more each year. "They've learned a lot. They've learned to work with people, about responsibility, and about networking," notes their teacher, Lynn. "The hands-on approach to learning has been tremendously successful!"

DREAM OF WILD HEALTH

Indigenous Varieties — Awakening to the 21st Century

The Dream of Wild Health is a traditional Native American garden project in the Upper Midwest. Its mission is to become the seed saver of indigenous American Indian plants in the region.

The Dream of Wild Health project began with dreams, the actual dreams of Sally Auger, of St. Paul, Minnesota. Sally recognized the decline of nutritional health of Native peoples and connected it to the loss of indigenous seed stock. She and the network's leaders imagine that Dream of Wild Health can slowly bring back nutrition as well as a rejuvenation of the culture.

The seed saving began with word of mouth "public relations" using the Pow-wow circuit. Dream of Wild Health is a collective effort to grow ancient seeds, carefully propagating them and bringing that genetic wisdom to light in the twenty-first century. "I have a feeling that this project is going to become very important; that we may be part of a change that is coming," says Sally.

Paul Red Elk manages the overall garden effort, along with Yako Myers, who helped design and now manages a Women's Medicine Garden. Here, perennial herbs and medicinal plants are grown in circular patterns, with ritual and deep respect for the gifts given by these plants for women's health. In the main acreage, the project workers are growing indigenous varieties of corn, beans, squash and sacred tobacco.

Seeds come from Native American gardeners all over the Midwest, and bear names such as: Quapaw, Mandan Red Clay, Cherokee Flour, Deleware, Arikara, Micmac White, Kickapoo Tama, Bear Island. Some seeds have been reunited with indigenous peoples from archeological digs, and are 800 years old. Amazingly, the 800-year old seed stock is germinating at excellent rates.

Cultural preservation is a big part of the picture for Dream of Wild Health. American Indian people have a rich tradition of gardening and using medicine derived from plant life, with which they have lived for thousands of years. As indigenous peoples' food sources changed — particularly with the onset of commodity foods on reservations — so, too, did the health of both their bodies and spirits. Today, more than fifty percent of the Native Americans in Minnesota live in the Twin Cities area, removed from their cultural traditions of healing and gardening.

The Dream of the Wild Health project creates an educational opportunity for the Native community as well as the non-Indian community. Paul Red Elk has been using photography to document plants and farming techniques, taking pictures of plants never before photographed. Residents of related organizations, Sacred Fire Lodge and Mother Earth Lodge, also help tend the gardens and learn about their own heritage. University of Minnesota nutrition science, biology,

natural resources and ethics students come to the garden to learn about pollination and native varieties. Native American youth-at-risk, from a group called Golden Eagles, have been involved making ancient tools of antler and bone, and have learned to use them in the garden.

A need for land with natural barriers to cross-pollination, labor for hand-pollination and careful propagation, and, of course, lack of cash are obstacles the Dream of Wild Health project has faced. Ironically, money is needed for this project, which seeks to preserve genetic traits, at a time when funding for genetic modification is at its height. Knowledge is also a limiting factor, since many of the seeds have outlived their original farmers. Many elders have limited memories of traditional ways, having lost them to missionary school educations and generations of living in urban areas. The very thought of growing medicinal plants is, at times, foreign to traditional Native thought. In the past, people gathered plants from fields and forests. Other Native leaders, however, were expert gardeners and horticulturists, and the traditions of gardening also run deep.

In the face of all of its challenges, the Dream of Wild Health's organizational spirit runs high. The organization uses what resources are available to accomplish its goals. Deeply respected elders have shared seeds and knowledge, recipes and ritual prayers. Seeds continue to come in, with stories about farming in traditional ways. This unique project is reintroducing native plants back to the environment, and at the same time, teaching people how to care for the plants and about the importance of this genetic material for Native peoples' health and for the Earth itself.

Work like this is important in restoring both ecosystem and human health. By bringing people from the city to the garden, bringing indigenous tribal cultures together, and young people together with elders, Dream of Wild Health is beginning a process of learning that will draw people into a closer relationship with the land. "When we planted fifteen to twenty plants in the first Dream of Wild Health garden in 1997, we weren't sure what would happen," says Sally. "The garden has grown beyond all our dreams, and the summer 2001 garden contained over 300 traditional indigenous plants. This year 800-year old beans and corn are germinating!" Collaboration is clearly evident in a braid of enthusiasm, hard work, and cultural responsibility as this project goes forward.

SCIENCE AND MATH SUMMER PROGRAM
Some Things You Can't Learn in a Classroom

For generations, the Ojibwe people lived off the land in what is now northern Minnesota. They harvested wild rice, medicinal herbs, and wild fruits, hunted and fished, collected maple sap and boiled it down into syrup, and built canoes, baskets, and seasonal lodging. Their way of life required strong analytical skills and a deep understanding of natural systems. In other words, they relied on practical applications of math and science to survive.

In recent years, many tribal members, particularly youth, have not followed these traditional ways and subsequently have not acquired the accompanying skills. Joe LaGarde, historian, explains, "Many children here (on the reservation) enter school convinced they will fail at math and science, and it often becomes a self-fulfilling prophecy." Elders on the White Earth Reservation were concerned with high dropout rates, a defeatist attitude among youth, and the lack of connection youth had to their cultural traditions. In the late 1990s, the community at White Earth responded to these concerns by creating the White Earth Reservation Science and Math (WERSM) summer program.

In this hands-on program, the youth explore the outdoors, take field trips, and discuss local natural resource issues. Guided by educators, natural resource professionals and elders, students learn how mathematics and science are used to understand and care for the environment. "The students test soils, sample stream waters and observe wildlife," explains Joe. "In doing so, they gain a greater appreciation of the importance of the environment to their culture, their lives, and the future of their community."

Students learn about gardening and plant growth. They test soil and water quality, take measurements of standing trees, sample streams for aquatic life, and learn about land use. In one session, students visited Ottertail River, where they collected water samples and learned to identify fish at a hatchery. On another field trip, they visited the Tamarac National Wildlife Refuge and Itasca State Park where they learned about wildlife biology, bird identification and conservation laws. Some students even accompanied Reservation biologist, Doug McArthur, as he rescued an injured trumpeter swan. "The kids here see practical science at work. You can learn it in the classroom, look at a book, but it really doesn't hit home until you get out here," explains Doug.

Elders and other tribal members, whom Joe refers to as "cultural advisors," are an essential part of the program. Along the way they teach the history and traditional uses of natural resources and their place in Ojibwe culture. For instance, during the exploration of a forest, a cultural advisor will tell stories about the forest and show kids what foods, materials, and medicines can be gathered. The youth will study the traditional role of fire in forest management and consequently learn the critical role of Native Americans in fire suppression efforts across the country. The students, working together

with the tribal dietician and elders, also plan and prepare a traditional feast for the community using foods found on the Reservation. Joe says, "By including cultural advisors as part of the program, the kids learn about who they are. The elders know the families on the reservation and tell the kids about their history."

The success of the program has been outstanding. Over seventy percent of participants complete the six-week session. In the first year, test scores rose

over one full grade-level in mathematics, and some students have expressed interest in pursuing higher education. The community has benefited from new gardens and a plan for a school recycling and composting system.

But the story behind the story deserves telling because it, too, is exemplary. The seeds for the WERSM program were planted when the Circle of Life school at White Earth partnered with Visions for Change (a Kellogg Foundation sponsored venture) to open a dialogue between White Earth tribal members and University of Minnesota faculty, staff, and students. In 1998, a bus load of faculty and staff traveled to White Earth Reservation and spent two days learning from the people of White Earth and discussing ways that the university and tribal members could collaborate.

The idea of a math and science camp was raised, and people rolled up their sleeves and got to work. The program evolved through a series of meetings during which the summer session planners got to know each other, developed a comfortable working relationship, discussed roles and cultural aspects of the education, and finally identified a curriculum. Critical to the process was a commitment by all involved that the program's development and implementation be rooted in respect and partnership. "There is a real respect for all kinds of knowledge and wisdom," explains Joe. "University faculty bring a certain kind of expertise, elders bring another."

Truly a team effort, the elders focused on the cultural perspective, a local natural resource manager (also a tribal member) focused on the tribal perspective, and the University of Minnesota team members focused on the logistics of the project. Funding for the initiative was also a team effort. The University of Minnesota Extension Service, the Circle of Life School, the White Earth Reservation Tribal Council, the Rural Minnesota Concentrated Employment Program Inc. (CEP), and Visions for Change provided the funds needed to launch the summer program. Now the partners are working to find permanent funds to continue and expand the program.

By helping youth examine their environment through both a scientific and a cultural perspective, the White Earth Reservation Science and Math Program reconnects Ojibwe youth with their own traditions, history and landscape. The elders hope the careful attention to tribal culture and community will increase the students' pride in their heritage. Joe says, "We hope the program has a long-lasting impact on the summer school participants and knits them closer to their community so that they carry the knowledge and strength of their tradition with them wherever they travel in their future lives."

YOUTH FARM AND MARKET PROJECT

Fostering Strong Roots in Urban Agriculture

In the United States, kids, especially city kids, are profoundly discon-
nected from the basic human process of growing and preparing food.
Food comes from a store — or drive-thru — and involves money
changing hands. The hunting, gathering, planting, tending, harvesting,
milling, and cooking of food are acts invisible, unimaginable, and
hands-off for most kids.

But not these kids!

Youth Farm and Market Project (YFMP) began in 1995 in the Lyndale
Neighborhood of South Minneapolis. City youth, ages nine through
sixteen, grow produce on garden plots in their neighborhoods. "While
you will also find them playing basketball and soccer, jumping rope, and
watching TV, for three days a week in the summer, these youth are
urban farmers," says Karen Lehman, YFMP's former co-director. They
till the soil, plant seeds, and fertilize, water, and weed their crops. While
they mostly grow greens for mesclun and braising mixes, they also
grow tomatoes, onions, strawberries, mint, peas, parsley, and flowers.

Growing the food is just half of the story. On Saturdays, the youth take
turns bringing their produce to farmers' markets in their neighborhoods
and selling their goods to their neighbors. On a typical Saturday, in three
neighborhoods in Minneapolis and St. Paul, the YFMP kids become
budding entrepreneurs. While they joke and play between sales, as soon
as a customer steps up to the stand, they are all business with "Hello!
May we help you?" The youth answer questions, weigh produce, take
money, give change, and politely thank their customers. "We really
work with the youth to help them build their skills and their confidence

in those skills," notes Molly Van Avery, the director of the Powderhorn YFMP program.

During YFMP's first year, there were ten kids involved in the program. They sold produce at two markets and made nearly $500 in sales. In 2000, there were 227 kids participating; they sold at ten markets; and sales totaled $13,000. Currently, YFMP has programs in the Lyndale and Powderhorn neighborhoods of Minneapolis and on the West Side of St. Paul. They have developed over an acre of urban farmland on land made available by churches, schools, public housing sites, and the city.

Of obvious importance to the success of YFMP is that the youth like the program. "It's fun!" says Lakisha. "My favorite part is when I help people," she adds. "I like working and meeting people," says Erick. And Michael, age nine, says, "I like the money!" The youth get a five dollar stipend per day for their participation in the program.

"YFMP's work has evolved from a focus on urban agriculture toward a more holistic focus on food and health," explains Karen. Take the Global Kids program, launched in 1999. By integrating farming and cooking arts from five cultural roots (Africa, Asia, Europe, Latin America, and North America) kids develop a more personal connection with the food they eat and gain a better understanding of their peers. Youth grow foods from these cultures

and then work with chefs and parents from these five traditions to learn about how different cultures use the food they grow.

Kids have cooked with local chef Lucia Watson in her Minneapolis restaurant, with Jenny Breen from the Good Life Café, and chefs from Chiang Mai Thai, D'Amico Cucina, and other notable Twin Cities restaurants. Youth developed their own cookbook under the guidance of parent volunteers.

Inspired by the positive experience, the kids now cook their own lunches as part of the program. Working with a cook and using their own harvest when possible, they take turns making a variety of dishes for the rest of the youth. Fare includes traditional Hmong and Mexican dishes such as tamales, rice soup, eggrolls, Fa Kao, enchiladas, and molé, as well as more familiar dishes like tacos and sandwiches. Youth explore and ask questions about the other cultures' cooking. "A kid will say 'I never thought I would, but I really loved those eggrolls!' or 'those tamales that your Mom taught us how to make were good — she's a great cook,'" notes Karen.

Bridging the urban-rural divide, YFMP also collaborates with Philadelphia Community Farm (PCF) in Osceola, Wisconsin and Wilder Forest in Somerset to give these YFMP city kids a rural farming experience. YFMP kids travel in groups of ten to the farms and spend three days learning to milk cows, make butter and yogurt, corral sheep, load hay, harvest vegetables, set up irrigation lines and make potting soil. They also cook their own meals, go swimming in the St. Croix River, walk in the woods at twilight, and have bonfires.

Like seeds germinating underground, the long-term impacts of this program are yet to be seen. These kids are gaining an understanding of food and nutrition that most kids, and many adults, lack. They also are learning useful skills about work and business. Who knows, maybe one of them will be the next great chef, choose farming for a profession, or be a successful business person. At the very least, these youth have a good time growing, selling and eating food. Through this program, YFMP plants and nurtures more than one kind of seed!

AFTERWORD

This wonderful book has a wonderful story. It started with a gift I received from a close friend from the Netherlands — a big, green beautiful book that told the stories of over 200 creative individuals and groups renewing the Dutch countryside. Jan Joannides, community activist extraordinaire, took one look at it and decided we had to do something like it in Minnesota. She knew of literally hundreds of people all over the state who were turning exciting ideas and hard work into new businesses, new ways of farming, new products, and new life for their rural communities. She saw this book as a way to honor them and inspire others.

Jan and I created a project at the Institute for Agriculture and Trade Policy (IATP) to turn her vision into reality. We decided to also create a website (www.mncountryside.org), knowing that there were many more stories than we could include in a single book. We knew a website would give us the ability to update stories and expand the project to other states.

Early in the project, the Great Plains Institute for Sustainable Development (GPISD) contacted us to discuss a partnership. Having come up with the idea of showcasing rural success stories on their own, they saw value in working together rather than duplicating efforts. It made all the sense in the world to join forces and soon Jan, IATP, and GPISD were collaborating on the project. Jan and Sara Bergan, GPISD's talented executive director, have led the effort to produce this book and website. They have had outstanding assistance from Wendi Ward, who served as the story contact manager.

Sara and the GPISD board of directors intend to make the Minnesota edition the first in a series for the whole region. GPISD is also taking the lead on expanding the Renewing the Countryside website. Joni Vincent, Ryan Tombs, and Josef Ling's genius have been critical to developing the web portion of this endeavor.

A number of others saw the potential of this project, but none so clearly as Okey Ukaga, executive director of the University of Minnesota Northeast Minnesota Sustainable Development Partnership. Okey brought this idea to his board of directors – who generously provided the first funding for this project — and he has been a creative force throughout.

The soul of this book comes from the stories of these amazing people who are showcased here. We were able to capture that soul on these pages through the extraordinary talent of a team of artists and writers. The art direction, design, and production of this book comes from the gifted hand of Brett Olson of Geografix. From cover to cover, Brett's artistry is evident. It is his talent that brought the many elements together and transformed them into a book that is both beautiful to look at and to hold.

Beth Waterhouse's writing and editing, including a number of stories and the essays that connect the chapters of the book, provide the magic and energy crucial to making this book both lovely and inspiring. Farmer, writer, and community activist Tim King wrote over a third of the stories for the book. Tim's amazing ability to capture the heart of a story and bring it to life is evident on these pages.

A number of others wrote stories for this project or allowed us to adapt an earlier piece they had written. These individuals include Laurie Allmann, Sara Bergan, Janet Berryhill, Tom Cherveny, Kathy Connell, Lisa Daniels, Sue Farmer, Cindy Green, Gary Gunderson, Jan Joannides, Jo Anne Killeen, Karen Lehman, Dan Lemke, Rick Moore, Andy Olds, Kira Pascoe, Dimitri T. Phill, Ann Schwartz, Joni Vincent, Steve Waller, Jennifer Walz, and Wendi Ward.

We also want to thank the newspapers and publications where a number of the stories were originally published. They include: *Ag Innovation News*, *Agri News*, *City Pages*, *Dairy Today*, *In Business Magazine*, *Lake Country Journal*, *Lakes Alive*, *The Land*, *Land Protection Options: A Handbook for Minnesota Landowners*, *Long Prairie Leader*, Minnesota Office of Environmental Assistance website, *Minneapolis Star Tribune*, *Small Farm Today*, *University of Minnesota Kiosk*, and the *Willmar Tribune*.

It is the photographs in this book that inspire many to pick it up and get lost in its pages. We were thrilled when Doug Beasley, one of Minnesota's most gifted photographers, joined the project. Doug spent numerous weekends on the road capturing on film many of the magnificent pictures you see here. When we were in a pinch to get all the photography done in time to go to press, Rick McFerrin, having recently returned from biking around the world with Tanya, his wife, hit the road again with Tanya and their new son Sampson, to capture more images for this book. Rick's photographs grace many of the pages of this book.

We are grateful to a number of other wonderful photographers, both professional and amateur, whose work is included on these pages: Meredith Anderson, Sara Bergan, David Benson, Ron Bowen, Don Breneman, Brian DeVore, Kristi Link Fernholz, Rolf Hagberg, Dave Hansen, Carrol Hendersen, Jan Joannides, Carl Nelson, Gary Alan Nelson, Brett Olson, O.S. Pettingill, Paul Red Elk, Mike Reichenbach, Ricardo Salvador, Anthony Brett Schreck, Peggy Sobczak, and Terry Vidal.

A number of organizations and agencies generously permitted us to use their photographs. They include the University of Minnesota Extension Service, the Agriculture Utilization Research Institute, the Minnesota Department of Natural Resource, the Land Stewardship Project, Windustry, Minnesota Project, the Trust for Public Land, the Cornell Laboratory of Ornithology, and the Minnesota Historical Society.

A whole team of individuals volunteered their time to do the final proofreading. We express our thanks to these individuals: Brian Corner, Les Everett, Olive Joannides, Karen Lokkesmoe, Kim Mason, Karin Matchett, Helene Murray, Beth Nelson, Emily Schlough, Mark Stewart, Joni Vincent, Wendi Ward, Bill Wilcke, and Kyla Zaro-Moore.

Financial supporters made it possible to turn this dream into a reality. We thank the Northwest Area Foundation, the University of Minnesota Northeast Minnesota Sustainable Development Partnership, the McKnight Foundation, the Surdna Foundation, the Experiment in Rural Cooperation, the Agricultural Utilization Research Institute, the Minnesota Institute for Sustainable Agriculture at the University of Minnesota, and North Country Coop for their support.

A special thanks to the whole crew at A.G. Johnson who printed this book beautifully, worked many late hours to meet our deadlines, and were very patient and accomodating in the process. We also thank New Leaf Paper for providing a source of environmentally responsible and economically sound paper. While not a Minnesota company, New Leaf Paper is an outstanding example of a company providing consumers with more sustainable options.

Finally, we want to thank the individuals featured in the stories and pictures on these pages who were the inspiration for this book. They were extraordinarily generous in sharing their stories and time with all of the writers, photographers and editors. We also want to thank all the other individuals and families working to renew Minnesota's countryside who we were unable to include in this volume. We hope to get each and every one of your stories on our website and in future editions of this book.

For more information about the stories in this book and about many, many more wonderful examples visit the Renewing the Countryside website at www.mncountryside.org. You will be inspired!

Mark Ritchie, President, Institute for Agriculture and Trade Policy

PHOTO & WRITING CREDITS

Cover Photos

front cover, from left to right

Autumn Countryside, photo by Doug Beasley, Beasley Photography

Snow on Pines, photo by Gary Alan Nelson

Audrey Arner and Richard Handeen, photo by Doug Beasley, Beasley Photography

Fields in Southern Minnesota, photo by Rick McFerrin, Two Wheel View

Painting at Harvest Moon Community Farm, photo by Doug Beasley, Beasley Photography

inside cover

Sheep, photo by Doug Beasley, Beasley Photography

back cover

Jim VanDerPol and grandson, photo by Doug Beasley, Beasley Photography

Introduction Photos

p. 2   Sunrise at Scherping Farm, photo by Doug Beasley, Beasley Photography

p. 5   Kneading Dough at Minnesota Camphill Village, photo by Doug Beasley, Beasley Photography

p. 6   Road in Autumn, photo by Gary Alan Nelson

p. 8   top row, left to right
Root River Market Sign, photo courtesy of Peter Denzer
Mississippi Headwaters Hostel Sign, photo by Rick McFerrin, Two Wheel View
Java River Sign, photo by Kristi Link Fernholz

p. 8   second row, left to right
Rural American Arts Sign, photo by Rick McFerrin, Two Wheel View
Angry Trout Cafe Sign, photo by Doug Beasley, Beasley Photography
Youth Farm and Market Sign, photo by Rick McFerrin, Two Wheel View

p. 8   bottom row, left to right
Prairie Restoration, Inc. Sign, photo by Ron Bowen
Round River Farm sign, photo by Doug Beasley, Beasley Photography
Camphill Bakery Sign, photo by Doug Beasley, Beasley Photography

p. 11, Olivia Olson Joannides, photo by Brett Olson, Geografix

p. 12   Minnesota Prairie, photo by Gary Alan Nelson

p. 13   Sunset at Angry Trout Cafe, photo by Doug Beasley, Beasley Photography

Farming - Chapter One

Introduction

written by Beth Waterhouse

p. 14   Fields in Southern Minnesota, photo by Rick McFerrin, Two Wheel View

p. 15   Woman Harvesting Crop, photo by Dave Hansen, University of Minnesota Extension Service

p. 15   Jim VanDerPol and Grandson, photo by Doug Beasley, Beasley Photography

Willow Lake Farm

written by Tim King

p. 16   Sandpiper, photo by O.S. Pettingill, courtesy of Cornell Laboratory of Ornithology

p. 17   Tony Thompson, photo by Ricardo Salvador, Iowa State University

p. 18   Wild Lupine, photo by Gary Alan Nelson

Pastures A Plenty

written by Kira Pascoe

p. 19   Hogs in Pasture, photo by Brian DeVore, Land Stewardship Project

p. 21   VanDerPol Family, photo by Doug Beasley, Beasley Photography

Round River Farm

written by Ann Schwartz

p. 22   Abazs Family, photo by Rolf Hagberg, Jeff Frey & Associates Photography

p. 24   top, Shalom Seed Sanctuary, photo by Doug Beasley, Beasley Photography

p. 24   bottom, Squash, photo by Doug Beasley, Beasley Photography

New Immigrant Farm Program

adapted from story written by Rick Moore and published in *University of Minnesota Kiosk*, June 2001

p. 25   Nigatu Tadesse, photo by Dave Hansen, University of Minnesota Extension Service

p. 26   Minneapolis Farmers' Market, photo by Doug Beasley, Beasley Photography

p. 27   Farmer Weeding His Fields, photo by Dave Hansen, University of Minnesota Extension Service

Peterson Family Farm

written by Tim King

p. 28   Sever's Market Stand, Peterson family photo collection

p. 29   Sever, Sharon, and Sever's brother, Peterson family photo collection

p. 30   Boy at Corn Maze, Peterson family photo collection

Scherping Family Farm

written by Tim King

p. 31   Cows in Pasture, photo by Doug Beasley, Beasley Photography

p. 32   Rodolfo Scherping, photo by Doug Beasley, Beasley Photography

p. 33   Scherping Family, photo by Doug Beasley, Beasley Photography

Marketing - Chapter Two

Introduction

written by Beth Waterhouse

p. 34   Minneapolis Farmers' Market, photo by Doug Beasley, Beasley Photography

p. 35   top, Wild Rose Farm Shirts, photo by Rick McFerrin, Two Wheel View

p. 35   bottom, Java River, photo by Kristi Link Fernholz

Whole Farm Coop

written by Tim King

p. 36   Marty Primus, photo by Doug Beasley, Beasley Photography

p. 37   Whole Farm Coop Delivery, photo by Rolf Hagberg, courtesy of Agricultural Utilization Research Institute

p. 38   Sales, photo by Rolf Hagberg, courtesy of Agricultural Utilization Research Institute

Dancing Winds Farm

adapted from story written by Dimitria T. Phill and first published in *Minneapolis Star Tribune*, September 2, 1999

p. 39   Mary Doerr, photo by Rick McFerrin, Two Wheel View

p. 40   Goats, photo by Rick McFerrin, Two Wheel View

p. 41   Draining off Whey, photo by Rick McFerrin, Two Wheel View

STORY CONTACTS

Following, in alphabetical order, is the contact information for the many of the enterprises and programs highlighted in this book.

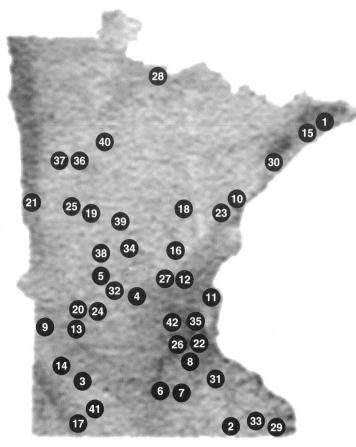

1. Angry Trout Cafe
P.O. Box 973
W HWY 61
Grand Marais, MN 55604
phone: 218-387-1265

2. Badgersett Research Corporation
RR1 Box 141
Canton, MN 55922
phone: 507-743-8570
website: www.badgersett.com

3. B.O.L.T. Enterprises
Westbrook – Walnut Grove High School
P.O. Box 129
Westbrook, MN 56183
phone: 507-274-6111
fax: 507-274-6113
email: boltent@westbrook.mntm.org
website: www.westbrook.mntm.org

4. Bresnahan Studio
Box 6377 Saint John's University
Collegeville, MN 56321
phone: 320-363-2930
fax: 320-363-2504
email: pottery@csbsju.edu
website: www.stjohnsuniversity.edu

5. Camphill Village Minnesota
RR 3 Box 249
Sauk Center, MN 56378
phone: 320-732-3925
email: cvmn@rea-alp.com
website: www.camphillvillage-minnesota.org

6. Centro Campesino
104 1/2 Broadway St. W #206
Owatanna, MN 55060
phone: 507-446-9599
fax: 507-446-1101
email: migrante@rconnect.com

7. Dancing Winds Farm
6863 Co. #12 Blvd
Kenyon. MN 55946-4125
phone: 507-789-6606
email: dancingwinds@juno.com
website: www.dancingwinds.com

8. Dream of Wild Health
459 N. Wheeler St.
St. Paul, MN 55104
phone: 651-646-8167
fax: 651-646-1665
email: odawa@skypoint.com
website: www.petawakantipi.org

9. Earthrise Farm
RR 2, Box 94A
Madison, MN 56256
phone: 320-752-4700
email: erfarm@hotmail.com

10. Harvest Festival
Sustainable Farming Association Northeast
DeWitt-Seitz Bldg #313A
394 Lake Ave S
Duluth, MN 55802
phone: 218-727-1414
email: sfa@skypoint.com
website: www.harvestfest.cjb.ne

11. Harvest Moon Community Farm
14363 Oren Road North
Scandia, MN 55073
phone: 651-433-4358
fax: 651-433-4652
email: hmcf@mailcity.com
website: www.hmcf.org

12. Haubenschild Dairy
email: hauby@ecenet.com

13. Java River
210 South 1st
Montivideo, MN 56265
phone: 320-269-7106
email: pjmoore@landstewardshipproject.org
website: www.prairiefare.com

14. Kas Brothers
Dan Mar & Associates
Djuhl@dtgnet.com or
Windustry
phone: 612-374-2261
email: info@windustry.org
website: www.windustry.org

15. Lutsen Scientific and Natural Area
Scientific and Natural Areas Program
Minnesota Department of Natural Resources
500 Lafayette Road, Box 25
St. Paul, MN 55115
phone: 651-297-2357
email: bob.djupstrom@dnr.state.mn.us
website: www.dnr.state.mn.us/
ecological_services/sna

16. Mille Lacs Indian Museum
43411 Oodena Dr.
Onamia, MN 56359
phone: 320-532-3632
fax: 320-532-4625
website: www.mnhs.org

17. Minnesota Certified Pork
Minnesota Department of Agriculture
90 West Plato Blvd.
St. Paul, MN 55107
651-297-1629
paul.strandberg@state.mn.us